Penguin Books
Nothing to Spare

Jan Carter was born and educated in Perth, Western
Australia. She has a B.A. (Psychology and Philosophy)
from Melbourne University and a M.Sc. (Sociology) from
Bedford College of the University of London. She is a
qualified social worker and has worked in hospitals in
Melbourne, Perth, and London. Recently, she has been
working as a freelance researcher, investigating health and
social services.

Jan Carter

nothing to spare

Recollections of Australian
Pioneering Women

Penguin Books

Penguin Books Australia Ltd,
487 Maroondah Highway, P.O. Box 257
Ringwood, Victoria, 3134, Australia
Penguin Books Ltd,
Harmondsworth, Middlesex, England
Penguin Books,
40 West 23rd Street, New York, N.Y. 10010, U.S.A.
Penguin Books Canada Limited,
2801 John Street, Markham, Ontario, Canada
Penguin Books (N.Z.) Ltd,
182-190 Wairau Road, Auckland 10, New Zealand

First published by Penguin Books Australia, 1981

Copyright © Jan Carter, 1981
Reprinted 1981, 1982, 1983, 1985, 1986

Typeset in Australia by Paragraphics Pty Ltd, Boronia, Victoria
Printed in Australia by The Dominion Press-Hedges & Bell

CIP

Carter, Jan
Nothing to spare.

ISBN 0 14 005824 9.

1. Women—Western Australia—Social conditions.
I. Title.

305.4'09941

For my grandmothers

Contents

Preface

This book records the memories of some Australian women who can recall the time from about the end of the last century until the First World War – from approximately 1890 until 1918. It constitutes a living record, for all but two of the women who contributed are living, but very old. On average, they are aged eighty-nine years and their ages range from eighty to one hundred. In this book they recall their pasts, through the lens of the present. The series of biographical cameos that result are sketched in the pages which follow.

A variety of influences contributed to this book. In the first place, I listened to the tales of two grandmothers, born in 1887 and 1897 respectively. In my childhood their stories seemed unremarkable, almost commonplace. But on returning to Australia, after ten years in London, my grandmothers' memories seemed to offer reminders of some of the social changes that had taken place during this century. In Australia, the conspicuous consumption and affluence of life in the cities of the 1970s, reminded me that there had been a time within living memory in Australia where life was lived as if there was nothing to spare. This book is an attempt to record this time.

Unwitting inspiration came too, from many old people in England and Wales. In conducting a national survey of day centres and day hospitals in England and Wales, between 1974 and 1979, I talked to a national random sample of old people. Interlaced between their accounts of their illnesses and their opinions about the services they received, were more interesting stories about growing up in Birmingham, Brighton, or Blackpool.

My questionnaire did not cope very well with these memories, but the experience did direct my interest towards the process of oral history. Although most stories in this book were recorded in Australia, perhaps my past informants in the U.K. and their descendants, will find occasion to compare and contrast their own lives with those of their Australian cousins. Now the main remaining cultural link between England and Australia is cricket: it might be helpful to remember a point in time when the ties were more obvious and the interdependence more crucial.

Friends in England and Australia have encouraged the development of this book. In particular, I need to thank those who introduced me to the women whose memories will speak for themselves. These include Margaret Clements, Jean Hamory, Margaret Jeffery, John Troy, Grace Vaughan and Leon Watt. Florence Binns has shown comprehensive interest and support; as well she typed parts of the manuscript. Marie Harris coped with untidy and illegible drafts. Jackie Yowell was positive and constructive about the project from the beginning and always available and Carla Taines has been a sensitive editor. The staff at the Battye Library in Perth helped me obtain most of the photographs used to illustrate this book. The Literature Board of the Australia Council provided a Special Purpose Grant to cover some of the expenses of the project. Then, the University of Western Australia offered me kindly refuge, as a Visiting Fellow in the Department of Social Work and Social Administration for part of the time.

The greatest thanks go to the women who appear in the book. We met as strangers and ended as friends. I would like them to feel that they have acquired one more granddaughter, or great niece. They were generous and patient and concerned. I hope they are pleased with the contribution they have made in reflecting on the lives of Australian women in times past.

Locations relevant to the text

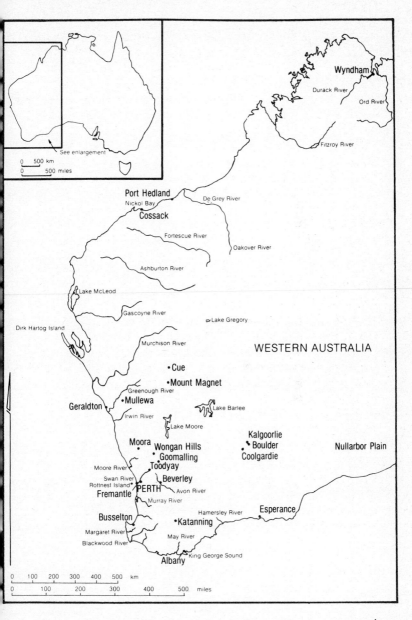

Veteran

Cataracts blanketed her eyes
at eighty, stretched an optician to impossible
magnification. An electrician made her corner
the brightest circle in the house.
Floodlit, she read and read.

Six months she wandered
backwards from a suburban bed to the small town
where she'd reared eleven. Three babies died.
'Blanchie take care of Archie
his first day at school.' All were recalled:
Flo Win Lil Kitty
Stan Jack Perce Annie Harold.

Sometimes my mother disowned me, spendthrift
frivolous, unmistakably her husband's child.
Then I claimed friendships well-turned
as roast dinners, people-yarns light as apple pies
the spicy air round my grandmother.

– Joyce Lee

Goldfields family, 1897

Introduction

In the 1890s the news of gold discoveries in Western Australia spread throughout the world and a stream of newcomers, mostly men, poured into the western colony, from the mother country, the Americas and 't'other side', as the eastern colonies of Australia were known. Within ten years the population of the colony trebled, while the lust of individuals for riches and excitement increased in ways that cannot be measured.

There is nothing unique in these circumstances. In California, for example, the 'forty-niners' rushed to the goldfields, after gold was found in 1848. About a quarter of a million people set up canvas communities and made and lost fortunes overnight. The lure of diamonds and gold drew 'rushes' to South Africa from the 1850s and in eastern Australia too, in the colonies of New South Wales and Victoria, these familiar patterns were repeated. Gold was found, there was an influx of migrants from all over the world and the locals downed tools and left the cities to look for gold. Most newcomers were men, and women in gold-rushing communities were scarce.

What *is* different about the case of Western Australia is that these events are still within living memory. With the possible exception of the Klondike rush, most colonial gold-rushes took place earlier in the nineteenth century. The opportunity of talking to their living witnesses has gone. But the living can still describe the 1890s in Western Australia and recall a past which will become inaccessible after their imminent deaths. For example, there is the miner's daughter, who died in 1979. She recounted her origins shortly before her death in the words which follow:

I was born in Melbourne in 1891 and two years after, Dad got the gold fever. He came out to the west for the cure and went to Cue, working in the gold-mines. He sent for my mother, my brother and me two years later, after he'd saved up enough money to pay the fare.

We arrived at Fremantle by ship and stayed at a big boarding house called 'Home from Home'. We caught the train to Mullewa and then the Cobb and Co. coach, an old-fashioned cab drawn by six horses. All luggage was piled up on the roof and there were eight passengers inside and us two children. It was a five-hundred-mile journey and we stayed overnight to give the horses a rest. The wayside house was all canvas, with an iron roof and run by an enormous woman, Mrs Sievewright. There was three beds in the room, four posts in the ground with canvas bags nailed across. Mother put my brother and I top and tail, mother took one bed and a lady took another.

Next morning the driver rounded up his horses and we set off for Cue. They were all bush roads and it was rough, like a ship. We arrived in Cue at night and there was crowds of men around the coach. This man picked me up. I remember him kissing me. I said to mother: 'Who's that man?' She said, 'That's your father.' I didn't even know my father!

Father took us home to a mud-brick house. (They used to make the bricks down the creek at the bottom of our house.) It was very comfortable inside, but no windows. There were shutters made of wood, and you had to push up the window with a stick under it to keep it open. At night you'd take the stick out to fasten the window down.

We lived in that house for years. There was only two rooms: the bedroom on one end and a big fireplace in the other room where we used to have our meals. Mum used to cook outside in a camp oven. There was no running water and the well was in the centre of the main road in Cue. You've seen Chinamen with their shoulder yoke and a basket each end? That's the way the miners used to get their water but they had yokes with kerosene tins!

I don't remember Chinamen in Cue, but there was nearly a street of Japs. I don't know what their men were doing, but the women were there for a Certain Purpose. We children weren't ever allowed down that street and as a child, I didn't know what it was about. I never heard mother and father discussing it and the women were never seen around the town.

Father came from a well-to-do family in London. (As a matter of fact, his eldest brother was manager of a Barclays Bank.) His uncle and aunt was going to tour the world in their ship and they took him on their tour, to cure him of wanting to go to sea. When they got to Port Melbourne, Dad left the boat and cleared right away to Echuca. He waited until the ship sailed and came down to Melbourne.

My father never went back to England. He met my mother working in a biscuit factory. Dad sent the word home to England that he had married a young woman he met in Australia. His father didn't know until they were married and he never met my mother.

Here are the stories of the life of women in Western Australia between 1890 and 1918, some of whom were affected directly by the gold-rushes. All except one were born before 1900. They come from a variety of classes and conditions: white and black, newcomers and old settlers, country and city, married and single. But they are ordinary women, ordinary in the sense that the circumstances of their early lives were unexceptional. They speak for themselves by recalling their memories of past times.

Recently, there has been an appreciation of the riches of the spoken word as a source of history. Words can supplement the information given in written documents but, as well, the spoken word can go further, for matters beyond the scope of the official records are discussed. Few ordinary people ever write autobiographies, so the spoken word can act as a history of everyday life, recording its detail and complexity as noted by those who would probably not write down their thoughts.

The women were not selected by a random sample, so it is probably not fair to infer that the lives of all women of the period were the same. But each woman provides a unique view of the way that her particular personal experiences were formed by the events of her time. How did the gold-rushes affect a family's upbringing? How did growing up on an outback farm affect the attitudes of a white woman to the Aboriginal people? How did the absence of men during the First World War influence the tasks and the outlook of the women who stayed at home?

The organization of this book is quite straightforward. At the beginning and end of the book is a discussion of the themes ('Introduction'), the historical and social background ('Context'), the implications and significance ('Retrospective') of the material, and the way the information was gathered ('Method'). But most of the book is taken up with the stories of the women. Although most of the story-tellers are happy for their names to be made public, two have asked for anonymity. So each woman will be identified throughout by reference to the occupation of her father. Of course, this does not say much – or anything – about the image each woman had – and has – of herself (after all, several came to reject their fathers), but it says a great deal about the background from which each came, the opportunities each was given and the niche each found for herself in adult life.

In fact, the stories make the point, implicit and sometimes explicit, that early opportunities were shaped considerably by the occupation of the fathers. And the order of the stories reflects the views held at the time concerning the relative importance of certain occupations when compared with others. So one finds that the daughter of the itinerant stockrider, whose story opens this book, sees herself at the bottom of the community ladder, while the bishop's daughter, who sees herself as others do, is at the top. And since there is, in this book, as in real life, a relationship between being poor, having a hard time and being unhappy, the reader will find the unhappiest stories at the bottom of the ladder and the beginning of the book.

The order of the stories does rather oversimplify the complexity of official rankings – such as in the census – of occupations of the time. Professional and higher administrative work was usually given precedence in any classification of jobs, including in the Western Australian Census of 1891. In other types of work, complicated gradings existed within each field. For example, all occupations connected with work on the land would go together and then be refined further, say from grazier to odd jobber.

But this is not a textbook, nor do the women come from families covering a complete range of occupations. So basically, the ordering of the stories reflects the points made by the women themselves about the social ladder of the time. Factors other than the prestige of the father's job have been considered. For example, there is the question of race: Aboriginal persons were not included in the census of the time, so the Aboriginal woman whose story starts the book did not even have a foot on the bottom rung of the official ladder. Another problem is how to classify a story where the head of the family was a mother, not a father. Her daughter's point about the tight restrictions placed on women's work of the time suggested that her story should come before the rest, since her foot on the social ladder was precarious. The rest of the stories follow on in an order which corresponds roughly to the rung on which the women informally assigned their fathers, on the basis of their understanding of the conventions of the time.

The book is directed to those interested in comparing life at the end of the twentieth century with that of the beginning. The period chosen begins and ends with features of considerable historical importance: in 1890 the colony of Western Australia achieved self-government from London on most matters, while the year 1918, of course, marks the end of the First World War. But the fundamental reason for choosing this particular period is arbitrary: some women still alive today can recall these far distant times.

Although the book is, in the main, a collection of stories, it sets itself the task of asking – and trying to answer – some questions. The first question is 'What did you do before the Great War, Grandmama?' Many Australian granddaughters and great-grand-daughters have listened to the tales of their grandmothers and marvelled at the social changes which separate their generations. If born in Australia, grandmother was born into a British colony profoundly isolated from the rest of the world. Communications with others within the colony were slow and time consuming, for although the telegraph had been invented, there was no telephone, radio, aeroplane, satellite. Whatever grandmother's station, she usually had to work hard. The soil was infertile and labour was short, so she often worked at men's tasks. In the house, town or country, she had little help with the physical effort required from her to care for her large family, for servants were not available in the remote areas. She felt out of sympathy with the Aboriginal people on whose land she lived, and distant from their way of life. These factors, to be discussed more fully later, were not peculiar to Western Australian women. But the experiences of women from that part of the world may strike chords for women in other regions.

A second question is about the way communities deal with the elderly. The women of this book are old – aged between eighty and one hundred years. Most suffer from a physical disability, or from poor health, and half of them are now in hospital because they can no longer look after themselves. Yet their memories are of a vigorous youth and this contrasts with their present fragility and dependence. Most of the women are lonely and feel forgotten and set apart from everyday life. Ageing has segregated them and left them without a part to play: their attitudes and skills are now regarded as *passé* by their great-granddaughters. What can be said about this present treatment of the old in the light of their past?

And a third question concerns what the lives of these women might say, if anything, to younger women today. Recently, a great deal has been written about the problems of women under forty, particularly those with small children who are said to suffer from suburban neurosis, or depression, or role confusion, or from countless other problems so labelled by sociologists or psychiatrists. They are said to have limited ways of expressing themselves, they have no one to talk to, they take Valium, they batter their children, they have nervous breakdowns. Yet, in material terms, most younger women are probably better off than their great-grandmothers, with more comfortable housing and devices that minimize the physical labour of housework; they can, if they wish, control their fertility and they have access to leisure opportunities which include the travel and sports formerly the perquisite of the rich. The paradox is that many of these great-granddaughters feel trapped and unfulfilled. What comment do the lives of their great-grandmothers make on their condition? Can we assume that hard work is a substitute for identity crises? Or that materialism corrupts?

So although this book is about a particular time in a specific society, it speaks to a wide audience. It suggests that the problems of women in one colonial community relate to the problems faced by women in other communities of the same time. It implies that women who are now forgotten and isolated because they have aged have powerful messages for us, when they are allowed to speak. They remind us that recalling the past is not only an act of nostalgia, but a force to be reckoned with when assessing the contemporary difficulties faced by their descendants.

When the first British people were sent to Western Australia from Sydney in 1826, no women were included in the small party of convicts and soldiers who landed at Albany, on the south-west coast, to forestall a French settlement and to investigate the possibility of convicts being sent from the east to the west coast. Neither had women been included on the earliest voyages of exploration recorded by Dutch explorers in the seventeenth century. And although Dutch trading ships had been shipwrecked on the western shores after being blown off course on their way from the Netherlands to the East Indies, no one knows the fate of the few women passengers.

In the eighteenth century there was considerable French scientific interest in the southern coasts of Australia. No women were likely to have been on board ship during these expeditions, but the Frenchmen recorded meetings with the all-male crews of several American whalers and sealing ships and commented on their depredations to Aboriginal women.

The first women settlers in Western Australia were, then, black. Those problems which were to become of such significance to white women – the extreme distances and the profound isolation, the infertile and ungiving soil, the difficulties of recruiting labour to work the land and the fear of hostile Aboriginal warriors – were not of much importance to the black women, whose preoccupations go unrecorded.

The first white women to come to Western Australia landed unceremoniously in 1829 on a small island off the coast, near the present port of Fremantle, after their ship caught on a reef. They formed part of a contingent preparing to found the Swan River

Settlement. The party of men and women settlers had arrived on two ships under the leadership of the Lieutenant Governor, James Stirling, and their primary aim was to take up land. The white founding mothers were the wives of middle-class settlers and soldiers. They and their husbands originated from London, or from cities in the south-east of England; many came from civil and defence service backgrounds, making them different from the convict women and soldiers' wives who arrived at New South Wales some fifty years before.

Paradoxically, these English middle-class white women found themselves living more like Aboriginal women than like the sisters and cousins they had left behind in Surrey and Sussex. Their vessels landed them on sandy beaches, where they set up tents and lived in sand. They lacked fresh food and shelter, but they had brought their pianos and chandeliers with them. As the Sutherlands, the Australian historians, wrote in 1878:

The colonists, quite unconscious of the future that lay before them, carried out great numbers of costly, very often unsuitable articles . . . It was found difficult to convey this property to the town and much of it was left to rot on the shore where carriages, pianos and articles of rich furniture lay half-buried in the sand and exposed to the alternations of sun and rain.

The lure of the Swan River Settlement for the early colonists was the promise of land. Land grants were sought eagerly by those escaping England in the wake of the Napoleonic wars and land was granted by the British government as payment for services, and as bonuses too – twenty acres for every £3-worth of goods imported to the colony. But the land remained fallow and the articles rotted.

From the beginning of settlement, the stage was set unwittingly for subsequent conflict about the control of land in Western Australia. The colonists' major purpose in emigrating was to obtain land: the Aborigines' spiritual *raison d'être* was their bond with the land. It is true that Lieutenant Governor Stirling wanted friendly relations with the Aborigines, but as Trollope commented in 1876:

It was impossible to explain to the natives that a benevolent race of men had come to live among them who were anxious to teach them good things. Their kangaroos and fish were driven away, their land was taken from them, the strangers assumed to be masters, and the black men did not see the benevolence.

Most colonizers of the Victorian period assumed that they were culturally and morally superior to the indigenous populations. The new Western Australians were no exception. For example, Lady Broome, the wife of the Governor, expressed her views on Aboriginal women in a letter in 1885:

You can easily imagine how impossible it is to get hold of the natives after they are grown up – for they are a very debased sort of savage – and to teach or civilise them in any way. So we chiefly look to what we can do for the children, to improve the condition of the next generation, and every effort is made to take the little creatures away from their parents if there is reason to believe them to be ill treated; but if the parents are kind, then many inducements are held out to the mother to come to settle near the children when she can see for herself that they are happy and well cared for.

The recorded attitudes of some of the early white women settlers to the Aborigines were those of repugnance and fright. Even though there had been no previous attacks on white women or children, Eliza Shaw, who arrived at the colony in 1830, wrote:

It is not safe for the white woman to be seen by them, as they are perfectly savage and would take women off by force if they could lay their hands on them: even female children are not safe to be alone . . . They are, particularly the women I am told, hideously ugly, but I have never seen them near enough to judge.

The arrival of the white women marked the beginning of a decline in the number of black women. By the end of the century, just seventy years after white colonization had begun, approximately 90 per cent of the total black population is estimated to have died from imported European diseases, or by massacres and killings.

While the adverse attitudes to native populations by British settlers of the nineteenth century were the rule rather than the exception, it is possible that the negative feelings of women settlers towards the Aboriginal people in Western Australia were compounded by the extreme isolation. Women were frequently left on their own with children in the bush for long periods. For example, there is Georgina Molloy, an early settler, whose husband, a former military man, took up land in 1830. She was often left alone with small children while her husband travelled on government and personal business. In writing to a dear friend in Scotland in 1833 from her beautiful but remote outpost on the Southern Ocean, Mrs Molloy commented: 'How would you like to be three years in a place without a female of your own rank to speak to or to be with you whatever happened?'

Of course, isolation is a psychological as well as a geographical fact and it is not the same thing as loneliness. That evocative tale of rural life, *Lark Rise to Candleford*, indicates that it was possible for a girl in an English village to feel lonely, while only fifteen kilometres from her family. But the eagerness with which the Western Australian women settlers fell on newspapers and letters from 'Home' suggest there may have been special qualities in both the isolation and the loneliness of living in Western Australia. Some of the settlers held holdings almost as large as some English counties, a factor which must have increased the technical problems of visiting the neighbours, consigning and receiving goods and services and soliciting help from others. After all, with a detailed coastline of 12 500 kilometres, it took nearly as long to sail from the south to the north of the colony as it did to sail from Perth to Sydney.

Distances in Western Australia were greater than in most colonial regions of the nineteenth-century world. 'Western Australia, that giant skeleton of a Colony', sniffed the historians Sutherland in 1878, was 'a vast region of unexplored wilderness.' A land mass of more than two and a half million square kilometres, eight times the size of the United Kingdom and larger than India, Western Australia was, according to a nineteenth-century colonial governor, 'the largest governed state in the world aside from Russia'. Another early visitor to the colony, Twopeny, confirmed the feeling of isolation: 'You feel yourself more out of the world in Perth than in Siberia.'

In the days when it took a sailing ship up to four months to reach Western Australia from England, the isolation and loneliness experienced by white women settlers was reinforced by their scarcity. Of those settlers arriving in the first few months of the colony's existence, only one out of every five was a woman. This imbalance existed for many years and at the end of the nineteenth century, there were proportionally fewer women in Western Australia than in the other five colonies of Australia. This contrasts with the United Kingdom, where there was a considerable surplus of women by the end of the nineteenth century. The imbalance there was, of course, partly caused by the emigration of men to the colonies.

The white settlers in Western Australia were unable to achieve instant harmony with the soil. They ignored the practices of their Aboriginal neighbours who had wrested a practical living off the land and its animals for centuries by applying intuitive ecological principles. Instead, settlers bemoaned their lack of success in transferring English crops and the destructive effects of poisonous native plants on their European livestock. Few of the initial middle-class landowners had worked on the land in England and they were novices without the background which had evolved from centuries of partnership between yeoman and soil in rural England. Ronald Blyth's study of the English village, *Akenfeld*, suggests that there was an atavistic thread between man and soil in rural areas of England, such as East Anglia, which allowed certain instincts, knowledge and emotions to be inherited from generation to generation, through unbroken contact with the life of the earth itself. But the middle-class settlers to Western Australia had ignored the wisdom of these realities and failed to note that the Aborigine sustained this link in Australia. They found the soil alien, and several early settlements had to be abandoned when the soil failed to produce. When Anthony Trollope visited the colony in 1875, he commented:

An ingenious but sarcastic Yankee, when asked what he thought of Western Australia, declared that it was the best country he had ever seen to run through an hour glass. He meant to insinuate that parts of the Colony he had visited were somewhat sandy.

13

Poor soil and lack of labour are, of course, allied problems. The white settler defined his progress in terms of his success in imposing European patterns of cultivation, by clearing the land and sowing. Since it was viewed as impractical to recruit Aboriginal labour on a permanent basis in the agricultural south of the colony in the early days, by 1849 the colonists had swallowed their middle-class pride and petitioned the British government for convict labour. So from 1850 to 1869, about 9500 British convicts were exported to the Swan River Settlement. One significant thing was that, unlike transportation to the eastern states of Australia, the Imperial government sent no female convicts to Western Australia. Reports of the degradation of many convict women and the sordid history of the female factories in the eastern states had reached Whitehall. But the transportation of male convicts only increased the imbalance between men and women in the colony. By this time, the social classes of the colony had broadened and in the interests of maintaining social order, the authorities were forced to consider the mating prospects of the non-propertied man. Said Trollope:

Women were sent out as emigrants, in respect of which great complaint is made by the Colony against the Government at home. It was said that the women were Irish and were low and were not calculated to make good mothers for future heroic settlers . . .

The scarcity of white women was connected with another aspect of the labour problem, the absence of servants. In most other nineteenth-century colonies it was possible for the ruling classes to recruit servants by training local natives in the ways of their masters. Charles Allen's account of the British settlements in India, *Plain Tales from the Raj,* notes that the English memsahib's strongest link with India was through the feudal relationship existing with her Indian servants. Sometimes these relationships survived passing generations. But the close relationship between white mistress and black servant, often male, of British Asia and Africa did not transfer readily to Western Australia. With the exception of the pastoral north of the colony, where Aboriginal women worked as domestics, there are few accounts of Aboriginal men or women in the nineteenth century as permanent servants in a household. A visitor from England in 1896, Lady Brassey, noted the absence of household help:

The difficulty of housekeeping here must be extreme. It is almost impossible to keep servants in the far away bush . . . I would earnestly advise everybody thinking of going to any out of the way part of our Colonies to learn to a certain extent how to do everything for himself or herself. Cooking, baking and washing, besides making and mending are duties which a woman may very likely have to undertake herself, or to teach an untrained servant to perform. I should be inclined to add to the list of desirable accomplishments, riding, driving and the art of shearing and saddling a horse in case of emergency, for the distances from place to place are great and the men are often all out on the run or in the bush.

Where white women were wanted in the colonies, then, it was primarily to work as domestics. 'Domestic servants must understand housework and not think they are going out to a life of idleness', advertised the Western Australian government in London. 'In a country where almost everyone is a worker, mistresses know what good work is and do much of it themselves.'

Qualifications for servants wanting to emigrate to Western Australia were spelled out in London in 1903 by a former governor, Sir Gerard Smith:

Domestic service in and around Perth, Fremantle and Guildford is in one sense, hard and in another, very easy. As a rule, very few domestic servants are kept. Three would be found to be comparatively rare. The great bulk of employers have two and of course in many cases only one. Thus there is plenty of work to do and not many to do it. At the same time, very considerable latitude is allowed in the shape of hours and liberty and occasional half holidays and wages are liberal.

Into this servantless gulf had stepped the nineteenth – and early twentieth – century British emigration societies. The predominance of numbers of men as against women was a matter of concern in most colonies, and in England there was an over–supply of women. Active export policies sent women from Britain to Canada, South Africa, New Zealand and Australia. First the British government and then a number of voluntary societies

15

were set up specifically to encourage the emigration of women, particularly impoverished gentlewomen. Many disputes of the time centered on the extent to which the gentlewoman, be she governess or lady help, could be asked to perform domestic duties.

By 1899 there were twice as many males as females in the colony, though there had been a steady increase of female newcomers to Western Australia during the gold-rushes of the 1890s. Women were either 't'other siders' (as recruits from the eastern states were known) or 'new chums' (from Britain). But new arrivals or not, these women found themselves in a paradoxical political position. Although completely unrepresented in economic and political life in Western Australia, they were given the vote in 1899. The adolescent colony had been given self-government in 1890, and before it joined the federation with the five other states in 1901, it set about imposing law and order on the transient and volatile miners. Relations between government and miners were tenuous, so enfranchising the women appeared to offer the government of the day stability and conservatism.

Most history is written about and from the point of view of men: the history of Western Australia is no exception. Histories describe economic and political events, in which women played no active part. In 1890, it was uncommon for the Perth newspaper the *West Australian,* to refer to women, except in highly selective categories. Women were mentioned most frequently in relation to their appearances in the police courts; their second most frequent notation came as a result of their participation at gentry social functions; third, they figured in the 'Situations Vacant' pages. So, the impression of West Australian women, based strictly on a review of the newspaper columns of 1890, was that they were drunks, prostitutes, vagrants or assaulters; flower arrangers, vocalists or brides; house and parlourmaids, governesses or tutors. The following tales help to amplify this restricted picture.

Australia is a free land,
Free without a doubt
If you haven't got a dinner
You're free to go without.

— Anon.

Miss Lock, the missionary who took the stockrider's
daughter to the orphanage, is in the centre.
Photographed at Carrolup Settlement, about 1915

When she was born, it was not the practice to register the births of Aboriginal babies. A policeman mounted on horseback rode around Aboriginal campsites, did a head count of children, and submitted an official return. So her birthdate needs to be estimated from her childhood memories. It is likely that she was born just after the turn of the century. She recalls the man with horse and cart who ascended lamp-posts each evening carrying a bucket, and as electric lighting was introduced in Perth in 1914, this gives some guide to the date.

This story enlightens our understanding of the predicament of Aboriginal families during the first part of the century. Repressive policies, enshrined in legislation, aimed to segregate the so-called 'half caste' or mixed-race child from his white counterparts. In practice, black children were frequently removed from their families and placed in missions; young people and others were confined to oppressively penal government settlements.

Now she is old. She lives, summer and winter, in a tent. Her campsite is on the fringe of the city and has few material comforts. Her assets are a folding canvas bed, a table and a chair, all on a rug on the dry earth. But she is not lonely; her husband is dead, but most of her nine living children and their families live at the camp. So her grandchildren play marbles around her feet and bring their dogs to visit her. Her people, led by one of her sons, are struggling to obtain land to live on so that the fragments of their abused and rejected culture might be salvaged. She is a key person in the discussions and meetings about these matters within her community.

Nearly blind, the stockrider's daughter is not able to walk very far on her own. She is a shy person who normally keeps her distance from outsiders: her experiences have taught her the value of this. But she is a warm, responsive woman with an alert and penetrating mind, a subtle sense of humour and a cultivated sense of the ironic. She is very observant and is able to paint a picture in words. Had she·been born a hundred years later in a society which offered equal opportunities to black women, what would she have become?

She has never discussed her past life with a person outside her own community before. She might have decided to remain apart from this book. As it is, she has shown a generous spirit in sharing herself with a stranger. This and her lack of rancour about the past are gifts, and I, as her white neighbour, feel grateful for them. Her story comes first because, as an Aboriginal, she remained outside the social rankings of the time. But in another sense, her story should come first in this book, simply because she was here first.

I don't know when I was born, except it was quite a long time ago. From what I heard of it, my people stayed in a camp and my grandfather was a teamster, he used to travel in the drays. He'd take the timber into Busselton, that's what I heard from me mother.

Before we was taken to the orphanage, we used to live in a tent behind an old homestead, which was where old Mrs Priest, lady Priest used to live. She had a daughter, Cecilia, and her son was Boxer. We camped there and that's where my father Nathaniel, old Nathaniel, used to ride off to work every day. He used to ride on a horse, backward and forward. My mother used to stay home. I don't think she ever went to school – them days, they didn't go, it wasn't worried about then. All my sisters lived there – Clara, Lena, Mabel, Dora and Maggie. I was the youngest. We had one brother, Tim. My older sister, Maggie, she used to go and work for this lady Priest. She'd do all the work for her, run the house. We used to stop behind in the camp, we were the only family there.

That lasted until we was taken by the missionary, Annie Lock. One day, she picked us up from Busselton. She took us away from there and put us in a home she was starting near Perth. She said she'd come to pick the children up and take them away to this home, where they can have schooling. And that was that. We had to get ready and she took us on the train.

Our uncle brought the missionary there. Our uncle Arthur, who was a busybody, had heard that his sister, Clara, my mother, had left my own father and left us. Our uncle would find things out and then go off and report yer, he was that sort of a bloke. Nobody didn't like him. All my older sisters, they hated my uncle for doing that to us. But we couldn't possibly stay with our father, because there was no one to look after us. When my father heard my mother was gone, he went to Pinjarra and asked her was she coming back. She said no, so he came back; they was finished then.

What happened was this: my mother, she got mixed up with another man. After my father used to ride off to work all day, we used to notice this other man used to come to the camp; he used to be seen there all the time, but I don't know what they was up to. When it was time for my father to come home, he used to go. That went on and on, until one day she said to my brother, Timothy and my sister, Dora, 'I'm going away on the 2 o'clock train today. I want you to carry my trunk up to the station.' When they come back, they said, 'You know that man what we seen here? Well, he was up at the station.' They caught the train away to Pinjarra. So that was that. Our uncle got to find out these things, so he brought the missionary there.

We wasn't too long on our own. Miss Lock come about a week after. Them days, those missionaries used to have a cape, a navy blue cape with one of those stiff collars on, a white holland dress, long, with an elastic belt around the waist; black shoes, lace-up ones, and a bonnet, shape of a horseshoe it was, blue velvet with a ribbon hanging right down. That was the uniform they used to wear.

She took us to this home in Welshpool, she had some more
children there and we stayed there for a while, then they got
this other place over in Victoria Park. There was about fifty
children, Aboriginal, in the home. We used to have plenty of
church. Going to church, backwards and forwards. Going to
school. I didn't go very far in school; them days, they'd go
until they was fourteen and they could go out to service then.

When we went out anywhere special, winter time, we had a
dark grey dress, red collar – flannel looking – and a belt
around, black shoes, black stockings. Red cap with black
stripes around it and red ribbons with bones here and elastic
underneath there. That was our uniform for winter. Summer
was a blue holland dress, straight up and down with white
collar and white straw hat on the head. When we had to go
down to church we marched in twos with a lady on the side.
Some of the white girls used to be cheeky – they used to sing
out when they saw the girls marching along: 'All the niggers in
navy blue.' Some of these girls used to come to church too,
you know, they were church people. They used to poke
tongues out and cheek the Aboriginal girls.

When I was in that home, I remember songs they used to
sing about Kaiser Bill. There was a big mob of soldiers there,
they had sunsets on their tin hats. When we seen them we had
to run. They used to call out 'Black Velvet', but we used to
take no notice. We could stand on the corner of the fence and
see their rifle range just where they'd fire on the target.

In this home they used to use the cane. Anyone who played
up, you'd have to go round and get the cuts. You were not
allowed to talk while you were eating. Talking when having
meals – you'd get the cuts on the hands, two on this hand, two
on that hand – cold mornings too! We used to cry and hold
our hands. All sorts of punishments: stand with your two
hands on your head, stand in the corner until they'd let you
go. When they weren't looking, we'd take our hands off our
heads.

They had an orchard at the home – fig trees and peaches.
The peach tree used to get us punished, you know; we used to

sneak out of the house, go underneath the tree and pull the peaches down. Wasn't allowed to do that – that was stealing.

There used to be a Mr Hunt, he had a biscuit factory. He used to give us biscuits at the home, all the broken biscuits. He'd put them in a wheat bag and when it was full, he'd send a message to the home for someone to go in and collect it. They used to have a big box and they used to tip them in and make them last. A handful of broken biscuits alongside your plate, everybody had them.

There used to be a tea room somewhere by the Grand Theatre. They used to give us cakes, the broken cakes. And when it was harvest festival time, fruit would be donated into the home. We used to have Egg Sunday, too; they'd pack eggs into the boxes and that was supposed to be a treat. Missionaries used to take us to church and on this platform out the front were all these things. Everyone used to be looking at us, you know. That's how we used to live in there, in that home.

The dairy near the causeway belonged to the Canning family. They used to donate the milk. The girls used to get ready after school and walk right to the dairy. And Mrs Canning always used to say, 'I haven't got much to give you this time' – it might have been only so much. We had to hurry back to the home along these old roads – we were scared and we'd run and sometimes the milk would spill. We'd get home and put it on the table. But we never touched that milk: it was put in coolers (no fridges them days) and used for the white staff.

The last I seen of Miss Annie Lock, she came to the home and said she was going to Alice Springs. She called us all up and brought us lollies and things. 'I'll be going to Kalgoorlie,' she said, 'and then I'll be going to Alice Springs on the camel train.' (I don't think them trains were going around then.) She said, 'I'm going to Alice Springs to start the mission there.' And she went; that was the last I seen of her. She must have died – she was elderly, even in those days.

I must have been about fourteen when they broke that

home up and sent us all down to the settlement at Carrolup River. I don't know why they sent us all the way down there.

At Carrolup, we wasn't allowed out of the compound. They had a big fence, all the way round: that was the compound. They was strict, we wasn't allowed to do certain things. We just had to stop in that compound. We were a lot of young girls and we had to have permission to do things. Like, Wednesdays, you could go for a walk; the sisters or one of the ladies that looked after us was allowed to take us. Then we'd have to be back. They used to lock us in the dormitories at night and in the morning; 6 o'clock, they'd open them doors and you could wash yourself and get ready for the breakfast then. You wasn't allowed to go for swims unless somebody was with you.

Some of the girls used to run away. They'd wait till they'd get their chance, then they'd duck off. But they'd soon be brought back: the trackers would go after them, some of them would be brought back and be punished. Never beating though – they'd put them in the cell, lock 'em up. They might be a fortnight in there. We was fed on bread and dripping for breakfast. I wasn't punished much at Carrolup. Only once I ran away with some other girls, we soon got caught, we didn't get far. Trackers got us. We didn't like them trackers – they used to watch what we was doing all the time. We wasn't allowed near the campies yet; we could stand at the fence and look down to the camp and see them moving around. Every Monday these campies came from the camp and you'd see 'em going past up to get their rations. Their ration was flour, tea, sugar and tobacco. Then you'd see them all going home again.

At Carrolup there was church. The priest used to come from Katanning, that was twenty-one miles out. He'd spend one night at Carrolup and then he'd go driving back in his sulky. At Carrolup, that's where we all got baptized in the river.

When we heard we was all going to be moved again they said: 'We'll have to get the priest out from Katanning and have your girls and boys all baptized.' So one day we had to go at 1 o'clock to the church; we had to march across the compound behind the priest and the lady missionaries. The priest held this big thing up, this cross thing. We had to all get into line in twos and twos and then we went down to the river.

First the priest walked into the water, up to here, he stood. And the lady missionary, she stood on the bank and as she read the names out, we had to go and get baptized in this river. The priest was standing there in the water and he'd say – what was it now? – 'In the name of the Father,' – *down* we'd go in the water – 'and the Son and the Holy Ghost.' Down, down. Deep it was, too! So we was all baptized there. Nobody kicked up much in those days, everyone came to church on Sundays.

I don't know why it was, but one day they came in and told us we was all moving again, up to the Moore River settlement. Police come out from Katanning and they said, 'We're going to shift yers.' You could see 'em supervising all the people, seeing that they was ready to go. No motor cars them days or trucks. Just the dray with the horse pulling it took us into Katanning police station. We all had to went there in the yard till 1 o'clock in the night when the train was coming. Then they said, 'You all got to get ready now,' and they marched us up to the railway station. The police was there to see that we all got on the train. We all got in the carriages. Lady Murphy, who used to look after us, was in there and there was a constable. He was on board on the train to see that no one ran away or got off. So that was that, we went, sitting in them old carriages with seats facing.

The train got to Brookton. They had kerosene buckets with tea in it and they'd brought boxes of bread. People could go and get some tea and bread.

Then we come on to Midland Junction. We got off and went to the railway yard. We all had to go and stop in there and wait for the next train. We was in there till the train went out, quite a long time. They said, 'While yers waiting, we'll put some pictures on for you in the Town Hall.' The silent

25

pictures, it was. If you couldn't read, well! – the ones who couldn't read just had to look at the pictures.

At the silent pictures, as they flashed the thing on, there was a man who used to sit playing a pianner, somewhere on the side of the wall when the pictures used to be flashed on, cowboys, horses and things. He used to play the music like the horses was galloping . . . That was the first time I went to a picture. We wasn't allowed to look at them, them silent pictures when we was in the home in Perth, that was very wicked. The missionaries said it was very wicked to go and look into a picture hall, you had to hurry along past it. Another thing that was wicked was never take money off a man or a stranger. They used to say we musn't talk to strange people. Drinking was never a thing though. They didn't used to worry about that. They didn't know nothing about that! – hadn't heard of it!

Anyway, after the picture, we went back to this big railway yard where we was all sittin', then march up to the station and all get on another train. We got up to Moore River, must have been about 11 o'clock in the night-time, got out, the train shunted off and we looked straight out onto the flat and all the camp-fires was in flame. The train that was shunted off left a few carriages – we lay all night on the seats in the carriages. The superintendent went off and slept in the hotel that night. Next morning, they come and said, 'All up and out of the train.' All the white staff got into this big buggy thing with horses pulling them. They called us all up and said, 'Now, there's this woman here, she has to look after you, you must do as you're told and all go to Moore River' – walking. That was eight miles out to there and when we got there they had tea and things ready for us. That's how we got to Moore River.

I might have been about sixteen then. I was in the sewing room again doing the buttonhole sewing until I learned to use the machine. The woman that was in charge of the sewing room used to be strict. Some of the girls used to get comics or reading books and put them in the machine, take the needle out and sit moving their foot. She used to whack the table and say, 'Haven't you finished those clothes?' If she found a girl out, that girl got punished. She reported her at the office and they sent a tracker over to get the girl. They'd take the girl away and they cut her hair off. They had a big iron thing which would cut your hair right off, bald. You weren't allowed to back answer the sewing lady, or do anything wrong, or that was your punishment. It happened to me, once, when I first learned to sew on the machine. I sewed the pants all wrong – the fly part, I didn't know how to put it on. When I took it up to the sewing teacher, she said, 'You know all this is wrong.' She went off at me and I back answered her, so she reported me to the office. The tracker came for me and I had to go over to have all my hair cut off, bald. I used to wear a hat; it growed again through. You used to get your punishment off 'em, all right.

There was one other punishment they had there. The man they done it to is dead and gone now. But when he was a young man, he used to run after this girl and go to the dormitory where she was. So they said we'll have to punish him. So they all went to the dormitory and stood inside and they tarred and feathered him; took his clothes off him, put the tar on him and stuck the feathers here. But I never seen that. They said he went out down towards the river like that, holding himself, then off into the bush and someone took him his pants and something to wash himself with. That was one fellow that got tarred and feathered for running one girl. He wouldn't keep away from her – he did after that.

They put people in the cells too for punishment. They had a 'boob' where you used to do fourteen days and the trackers would bring you whatever there was to eat; water and things, you'd stay in there until the fourteen days was up. No windows. The door was padlocked outside. That was for running away, playing up and cheeking the staff. You get used to everyday going on like that.

I might have been about sixteen then. They used to have all the married people in their houses down outside the compound and they had to stop there, outside. We in the

compound wasn't allowed to go outside unless we had the
sisters with us. We girls had to go to surgery and report and
put our names down every time we had a period. We picked
the 'squares' up and took them and used them and when we'd
finished we had to wash them all out and roll them all up
again. They put their name tag on them and put them in the
surgery.

Some of the girls, the older ones, they was allowed to have
boyfriends. They was allowed to go and talk with them. The
superintendent said they could talk with them. Those ones
what was getting married used to be allowed to sit out on the
office verandah and talk to their boyfriend. Sometimes they'd
get married – the rector from Gingin used to come. They had
their banns called once a month and when that was finished,
they had their wedding arranged for them. We had to go to
the wedding, everybody went and watched at the church.
Some used to have a wedding breakfast, they invited various
ones to go.

There was a lot of girls at Moore River, had been out to
service, different places they were at and they misbehaved
themselves out and they'd get pregnant. Well, they'd put them
back in Moore River to have their babies. There was one big
dormitory, the mothers' ward, where they'd stay till they had
their babies. No one else was allowed to go there. They'd stay
twelve months and then if they was lucky, they'd get another
chance, if someone was willing to take the mother and the
baby.

One girl there, she got pregnant, she was a Catholic and she
wasn't allowed to go to the church service. The Father used to
come out every month, to hold a service, confessions and that.
And she wasn't allowed to go to the church, she was not
allowed. She was pregnant; they just cast her off. She got
married after, but she was not allowed inside the church to get
married, she had to stand out in the porch, that was the rule.

At Moore River, they had a midwife. In a bad case, they'd
get an old doctor from New Norcia: some say he was a horse
doctor! He'd come along in his buggy. They had the hospital

right along side where the school children used to go past . . .
This poor woman was having this baby and she couldn't have
it, so they had to send for him. She was screaming the place
down and all the children were saying, 'I wonder what's goin'
on in there?'!

There was that protector from the Aborigines Protection
Board, A. L. Neville. I knew him, nobody liked him. Because
he was all for taking the children away from their parents.
He'd travel around the reserves and see the reports from the
police. 'Certain families are making a nuisance of themselves'
or 'they can't look after themselves.' So he goes to the police
station and looks at the complaints and the police warrants
and took the families away, into the settlements. That family
would be put in the settlement, they'd just be put there. The
police could be mistaken, but once in the settlement the
family gotta stop there until the native protector gave them an
O.K. to go out. When he comes on those visits, the people
could go and talk to him and if you could satisfy what he's
thinking, he'd let you free, that sort of thing.

He'd find you a job: 'Would you like a job out in service?
There's a lady wants a girl for service.' She might be in
Meekatharra, but if she wants a girl to help her, well, that girl
would have to go. She'd have to go there and work. If she
didn't want to go, she'd still have to go. Sometimes they'd
settle down when they got there, with the other girls.

Some ladies used to like to have Aboriginal girls working for
them. My sister was one what went out to work in Katanning.
She used to get 5s a week, 2s 6d pocket money and 2s 6d to
be sent away to the Aborigines Protection Board. We didn't
get paid for doing sewing either. They reckon they did after
we left the settlement – they reckon the girls were getting paid
for the sewing – but we didn't get anything.

I got married to get away from it all. He was at the
settlement too. We hadn't known each other too long. We left
the settlement and went to Toodyay – there was a job there. I
don't remember how old I was then – I did have my marriage
papers, but I lost them on the bus one day. I think I was

about sixteen. My sister was married to a bloke and working on a farm; he was a manager, he used to look after the place, so we went there. Mostly clearing jobs and post cutting, all that sort of job. We lived in a camp, where people was who give you the job (you could make a camp on their property). We had dogs to go after kangaroos, we had tea and sugar. I used to go to work, washing and scrubbing round the town, the women in town would want someone to go and do their washing.

We had friends in the town, people who, you know, liked to talk with Aboriginal people. Some used to go over the same old things, arguing over black people and white.

I never seen any bad feeling though. But Italians and all sorts of men, they'd get to argue about the Aboriginal. It's an old cry, the land belongs to the Aboriginal – even in those days they reckoned it was their country and the white people shouldn't be here. They'll never change that I think. Aboriginal people even then knew it, it was still theirs, it was their . . . *feeling* . . . that this was their country and they should be able to do what they like in it.

After Toodyay we came to Perth. My husband used to work and with that money we used to buy our bit of food and our clothing. But when we came to Perth, there was no work. I used to go and do washing and scrubbing for the women and I got a bit of extra money for doing that. My oldest boy used to go out caddying on a Sunday all around golf links. We went to Swanbourne, picked out our place, put up our tent and camp things and just lived. Just in tins mostly, we used to live under tins. We found the tins mostly from around the tips. You'd get the tins and make a camp to shelter from the rain and if you got good tins, you'd be right. You could build it however big you wanted it. We didn't have furniture; we'd only just have our rugs and mattresses and that was all. The table was unheard of! Pots and billycans to boil our tea, plates to eat off, but share them around. Toilets we built out of tins.

The Protection Board give you rations that was £2-worth. It was only so many ounces of salt, so many ounces of tapioca, so many ounces of sugar, tea and a meat order. Then you'd go to a butcher and he'd give you whatever *he* wanted to give you – any meat he can't sell, I s'pose that was it. We used to go and get the ration order and take it into John Wills, the grocers, in Perth and say to the bloke at the counter, 'Can you change this order?' And if he was a good sort of bloke, he'd say, 'Yes!' He'd say, 'Now what do yer 'ave?' He used to change it, they'd change the rations, but they weren't supposed to, so we could get what we wanted! Meat the same. Some would refuse you, they'd say no, we couldn't do that!

We stayed at Swanbourne till we got sick of it. Sometimes we went grape picking. Children weren't forced to go to school. But we made up our mind to come down here and we been here in Perth ever since, moving about. We walked around all the time.

Aboriginal people, they are not selfish sort of people; if that bloke over there has got nothing to eat, he can come over and eat here. If we have got something here, this one here will see that one there with nothing and will get up and ask him, 'You had anything to eat?' 'No.' 'Well, come over there and have something to eat.' They share what they got. They're different people.

I wasn't brought up with my mother's care – I was brought up by the white people, in the home, the orphanage. And my father only came to see us twice. Then he went back to Busselton and he died down there. I never ever could be with my parents, I was brought up the other way. You don't know what might have happened if I'd stayed with my parents down there – I mightn't have been sitting here today. The one thing was, we never forgave our uncle for putting us in the home – he was banned for putting us in the home – all his nieces hated him. We banned him for that and when he came to the home to see us, nobody wouldn't speak to him. But in the long run, I think . . . he was right. In the *long run*, after we could all think back, I think he was right by putting us up in that home. Because I don't think anything would have come of us being there . . . with our mother gone and our poor

father. And if it hadn't happened then, it might have
happened later: because this old Neville, this 'Protector', he'd
travel around. Children had to be taken from their mothers
and put into a mission . . . I don't know what they was trying
to do to us . . . as soon as they got old enough, they drifted
back . . . They'll never change, I don't think, . . . the Aboriginal
will always go back to his lot.

We were brought up away from home so I don't believe in
that Aboriginal thing – you hear a lot of talk about if they
don't like you, they can go away and 'sing' you; 'sing' you to
make you pass on. I don't believe in it. But a lot of people do
and they reckon they can do it, too. A lot of Aboriginal people
say they can see dead people and that, but a lot of my people
are dead and I never ever seen them. But I believe in God –
I been brought up on that, to believe there is a God. I don't
believe a person can come back – once you're gone, you're
gone. But my sister has told me that for Busselton people,
their spirits always return to Busselton after they die and travel
through the caves to live in the sea. So the spirits of Busselton
people always live on in the sea.

The barmaid

A Love Song for a Kalgoorlie Barmaid

Do you ever dream, my sweetheart, of a twilight long ago,
Of a park in old Kalgoorlie, where the bougainvilleas grow,
Where the moonbeams on the pathways trace a shimmering brocade,
And the overhanging peppers form a lovers' promenade?

Where in soft cascades of cadence from a garden close at hand,
Came the murmerous, mellow music of a sweet, orchestral band.
Years have flown since then, my sweetheart, fleet as orchard blooms
*   in May,*
But the hour that fills my dreaming, was it only yesterday?

. . .

Let them say it, dear, but oft-times in the dusk I close my eyes
And in dreams drift back to where the stars rain splendour from the
*   skies,*
To a park in far Kalgoorlie, where the golden wattles grow,
Where you kissed me in the twilight of a summer long ago.

— attributed to Herbert Hoover

Japanese women, probably prostitutes, on the goldfields, 1900

Hotel, Coolgardie, 1897

When the barmaid's daughter was born in 1900, the fever on the West Australian goldfields had just subsided and the gold town of Kalgoorlie, on the rim of one of the earth's largest deserts, had spawned the conventional trappings of Victorian civilization. Grave and stolid public buildings, fashionable women and frivolous entertainments were to be found in the town, surrounded by the flat red earth and dust storms.

At this time, the outstanding shortages in Kalgoorlie were water and women. So baths cost 2s 6d and the red-light district flourished. Engineering insights solved the water scarcity and a pipeline connected Kalgoorlie to a weir nearly five hundred kilometres away. But the scarcity of women was not so readily solved: in fact, emigrant women were advised to keep their distance from Kalgoorlie. A former state governor advised a London audience in 1902: 'The goldfields are not the place in my opinion for any woman under the age of twenty-five or thirty.'

The goldfields were not a conventional nursery from which to develop an ambition to work on the stage. But the barmaid's daughter moved to London after the First World War. She stayed in England, married and had two children and sixty years later she lives alone in retirement, confined to the ground floor of a house in Hampstead with her reluctant memories. She is deaf and badly crippled with arthritis. Classified by her local council as 'housebound', her occasional sorties to the outside world are by wheelchair. A home-help comes to help her with her washing, cleaning and shopping. She reads widely, has visits from old cronies and takes a lively interest in London gossip. Rather uncomfortably, she recalled her origins one cold, dark, December afternoon, as we looked out onto the garden where the Japanese tree blossomed unseasonally through the snow.

I never wanted to go back to Australia and I don't want to hear about it. It's at the back of my mind, and that's where I want it to stay. I couldn't wait to get away from the place – I expect it's all very different now.

I think my father must have gone to Kalgoorlie first. He was a gambler, and he and another man, my mother told me, found scope to start importing soap to the goldfields. Then he caught typhoid fever, as so many men did from the open drains, so my mother was widowed before I was six years old and left without money. Women had to earn their living: my mother became a barmaid. I heard that my mother was not very successful as a barmaid; she had to have a boy or a youth in the bar to protect her because she was so nervous. And she got the sack in her first job, because she was caught washing her hands with gin! It was supposed to whiten the hands – she was a very vain woman and beautiful.

I remember later on that I was dreadfully ashamed of her being a barmaid, but that was the way that women earned their living. Not every woman was educated to the extent they are now. Barmaids – handsome young women – were imported to the goldfields from New South Wales and Melbourne and there were some *lovely* creatures there. I was too young to know the details, but money would be paid for their passage. If they met a man on the boat – which they often did (they were so very well dressed) – and broke their contracts, their patron had to pay up for what it cost to bring them there.

The fashionable barmaids had followings in the bar. I remember one whom I liked very much, an Irish woman, Bourkie, they called her, she was very popular. As a child she made an impression on me. She had a lover who had a wife already and she had a big following. I remember hearing that

some man who was very prominent had a broken leg or
something and he'd said he'd sat and talked to her until he'd
forgotten all about the pain. When I was older, I saw her
again: she was no longer beautiful, she'd taken to drink. Her
face was all puffy, I remember what a shock it was to see her.

In the early days, women were generally barmaids if they
had nothing else they could do and if they were attractive. I
suppose you had to have *some* ability because you had to
count the drink out. But it was really being good-looking. You
see, it was really a form of prostitution, the women were
supposed to oblige the men. If pressure was put on some
women to keep their jobs, they became . . . willing victims . . .
obliging the men customers. Women held their jobs better if
they were obliging. It's the same now in certain walks of life.
Sometimes the barmaids were sacked if they weren't obliging,
not if they weren't efficient.

The well-to-do people lived well. There was the Great
Boulder Mine and other mines and the managers had a sort
of tradition. I remember going one day and having nursery
tea like they used to have in England. That was quite new to
me: I remember feeling very put out at being sent to have
warm milk with the children.

The races were popular and the women dressed beautifully.
They even imported clothes from Paris for the races; the
standard of elegance was very high. Practically all clothes were
made to order then, so women would dressmake. They would
also work in a store and there were good saleswomen; they
made a living that way and also had a following if they were
smart.

I was sent off to a boarding school in Perth. They had the
big boarding schools – the Methodist Ladies College and the
Girls' High School to which I went later on, because the
Church of England Sisters Boarding School, to which I went,
was quite austere. They were short of mattresses and we slept
on the beds – the standard of living was low. My mother came
to see me – she didn't often as the fare from Kalgoorlie was
beyond her. She came to take me out for the afternoon and

when she came up to where I was sleeping, she took me away and never took me back again. The bed was without a mattress and the big girls used to wave things on the end of hat pins and they must have been bedbugs.

I went to another boarding school, a girls' high school that was better in every way, including the food. The house looked over the Swan River. In the summer it was hot; we used to roll our mattresses up and take them out onto the balconies. There was a boat which took people on night trips up the Swan River, which was a brackish and wide river, with black swans. The boat had a searchlight and they flashed it. We thought we were very daring if we lifted up our nightgowns and put our bottoms towards the flare. I don't suppose they could see us, even!

The school was insistent that we had so much physical exercise. There was a recreation book: you had to report in this book how much exercise you had done through the day. You went for the awful crocodile walks, or you played tennis or had gym. We had a man named Sergeant Emmett who used to come for drill. He carried a strap in his pocket which he carried on to the Christian Brothers' and the boys' grammar schools!

The education was good. I was well educated even though I left school early. The headmistress was a woman called Melina F. Parnell – M.P., you see, for short. She was an Irishwoman, who had a B.A. and she was a musician. Only the best music or the most talented girls were taught by 'M.P.' Other people have told me that the standard of music was pretty low, but the school was proud of it. I had no musical abilities whatever.

I'd always wanted to be an actress. I played the baby in a French play before I was six – a scene in a railway carriage. I always remember my first speech: 'Bébé bébé voudrait chocolat', and I had to keep saying that non-stop; there were no cues. Then I got a prize for writing and Bishop Riley came up to Kalgoorlie to give away the prizes and the gels all went up and gave this little bow – one foot behind the other. I didn't think this good enough. When I went up to receive my prize, I put one foot behind the other and curtseyed down to the ground to show them what should be done. The bishop bowed back!

I was *precocious*. People used to think I'd do this, that and the other, but I had to leave school when I was young. There wasn't much family life – my brother was boarded out and my mother was trying to earn a living in Kalgoorlie.

At school, the pupils were very snobbish. The great idea was to get to England and be presented at Court. But I'd always wanted to be an actress. People took courses in shorthand and typing to fit them for jobs. I went to the technical college in Perth, for stenography and obtained a job in an office, before I turned fifteen. I had a job in the office of an English mining engineer, whose Board of Directors was in England. I didn't use the typewriter well. I was always being called to book by the accountant; I wasn't allowed to take things straight in to the boss which annoyed me. In 1914 the war broke out and I was living in a room in Perth somewhere.

Women didn't have many opportunities, there weren't many jobs available. There was a terrible system. When a girl couldn't do anything, she went as what was called a lady help, which meant to be treated as one of the family and sometimes that was unfortunate from the family's point of view, if there was a bloke there! She went up onto one of the stations and she generally got off with the eldest son or any young man about. The servant girls were of an uneducated class. Girls of fifteen and sixteen needed board and lodging so were sent off by their parents to do a certain amount of work; they only got about a pound a week and that was good pay.

I used to do odd jobs out of hours and I gave elocution lessons at two bob a lesson and saved the fare to Sydney – it was only £11 then. I'd sent photographs to J.C. Williamsons, the great theatre company. Their agent in Perth gave me an introduction to head office and they sent a letter and said to come.

So I went over to Sydney. I couldn't sing and I couldn't dance so the manager said, 'She can be an extra; she's got good height and good eyes.' Being an 'extra' meant you couldn't sing and you couldn't dance – you were just a handsome, tall girl. That's all I was at thirty bob a week, but at least I was that. I had to learn concerted movements. I did learn the various movements ultimately, but I was never quite in time or tune. I remember the ballet mistress, a severe woman, coming to me after the show opened and saying, 'As for you, miss, you're an eyesore to me from the front!'

Then I went back to shorthand, a firm of influential lawyers. I borrowed the fare from the senior partner and had my mother and brother over to Sydney and we lived there for a time. My mother had sent my brother up to the bush – to the north-west on a big station where he was very badly treated, physically beaten and so on. He became a roughrider; then he joined the Light Horse Cavalry when he was fifteen and went to the war. My mother should never have signed the papers to let him go at that age. He was in the entrance with Allenby into Palestine.

I wouldn't say the theatre was in my blood; I wasn't very good but my wish was still there. I came to London in 1924. I married an actor – that's his photograph there, playing Caesar on his horse. He was from World War I too and he had lung problems. He had a whiff of gas, but he lived until he was seventy-five which wasn't bad.

I never think of those Australian years now. I never wanted to go back. I never want to read anything about it – I had a hard time there. Once, in the twenties, I was at the Regent Palace Hotel in London, and I spoke to a friend. A woman came up and said, 'Excuse me. Are you Dorothy Fisher?' Her son, who was practically blind, had recognized my voice. He had heard me playing Tyl Tyl in *Bluebird* in Australia. The woman said, 'How changed you are. The last time I saw you, you were so thin with hollow cheeks and deep, dark eyes. You look so much better.' It's strange to be hungry in Australia and yet I was hungry, for years. There's nothing more to say about it. I can't think of anything else to tell you.

Father is the butcher
Mummy cuts the meat
Pussy rocks the cradle
While the baby sleeps.

– Anon.

Butcher's shop, Coolgardie, 1895

The Butcher's Daughter 4

A country woman for most of her life she was born in 1899 and spent most of her childhood in the gold-mining town of Yalgoo, about five hundred kilometres north of Perth. After she married at the age of sixteen, she moved around the bush with her husband who was a labourer on the railways. She spent many years of her married life living in tents in remote areas and had most of her seventeen children, all of whom lived, alone in tents.

Now divorced and an octagenarian, she lives alone in a small flat owned by the state housing commission in the port town of Fremantle. She cultivates house plants, crochets lace tablecloths and goes to a dance every fortnight at the railway station. She does not see much of her fifteen children still alive, apart from two sons.

The story of the butcher's daughter raises the question of the expectations of women about marriage. Although intelligent and able, many country women were handicapped by a poor education and entered into marriage young and unprepared, but accepting of its burdens. No formal and little informal preparation was offered young people prior to marriage. The evidence of historians such as Branca and demographers such as Borrie suggests that knowledge about marriage matters such as birth control was widespread by the beginning of the twentieth century, but such information was probably the purview of the literate who lived in cities. The daily newspaper carried advertisements in the 1890s for a booklet concerning the 'Physiology of Marriage', but as detailed information was sent by mail order, this service was obviously restricted to those who could read and write and those who were in touch with the daily press. The poorly educated and

Dryblowing gold, Pilbarra, in the 1890s

isolated country woman, out of the sphere of woman's organizations
and newspapers and magazines was at a disadvantage. As the
butcher's daughter indicates, there was very little information
available about sexual matters. Her knowledge of anatomy,
gleaned from diagrams in a medical textbook discarded by a
country doctor, is probably an isolated initiative in getting
information.

Other women have spoken of the agonies accompanying
marital ignorance. 'I lay on my bed at night on the verandah,'
reported the miner's wife, 'and pretended I was asleep. Night
after night, year after year, I would pray he wouldn't want to come
near me. It was horrible. When I could hear him snoring in the
next bedroom, I knew I could relax.'

I've had a blackfeller's life, I reckon. I was born at the
lighthouse, near Geraldton, 1899. My father happened to be
working there at the same time; then he went to butcherin' in
Geraldton. I was the eldest of eight children – we all lived. We
left Geraldton and went to Yalgoo when I was four. We went
by train, I'll never forget that. Dad met us at the station and
took us up to a hotel for breakfast. I couldn't make it out, you
know, all those tables and people comin' and puttin' things
on 'em. We didn't know what it was all about, our eyes nearly
popped out of our head.

There was a house at the butcher's shop, we went there.
Dad was the only butcher in Yalgoo. He used to have to go
out to kill the meat himself; he had his own slaughterin' yard
about four mile from town. His boss used to buy the cattle
and sheep, they had paddocks they used to keep 'em in. And
the slaughterman used to go out and fetch in so many of what
he thought was wanted; he used to fetch in a bullock every
Friday then.

The meat didn't last as long in those days. They used to
keep it in great big coolers – water coolers. They'd make the
frame and cover it with hessian. They'd make a big tin tray

and put it on the top of it and they'd have pieces of flannel comin' out of the water to fetch the water down the hessian, and that was to saturate it, then a draught was blowin' through it. The butcher's shop was a wooden only place, but the meat would keep for several days like that.

My mother had to work because my father had to leave the butcherin' business, on account of the blood. He got sick: he was off work for about five years, he used to have to go back and forwards to Geraldton for about five years. It was something to do with his liver and the blood was gunna kill him! Don't really know much about that, just what I've heard since.

My mother had to work all the time, she had to work every single day: cooking, washing, ironing, cleaning – anything she could get. She used to work for the storekeepers and she used to go to the hotels, cooking. There was five hotels in Yalgoo at that time – she used to go to one and work for a certain time there. She was away all day; I used to knock up some tucker at home – we'd make up a stew or a curry, same as what we'd have now. We used to grow our own vegetables.

From when I was about eight, I used to go home from school, put the horse in the spring cart, get the two dogs and go out in the bush, to fetch a couple of kangaroos. The dogs would get the smell up of the kangaroos and want to get out of the cart. I'd let the dogs out and they'd fossick around until they found them, then they'd fight with them till they killed them. They used to bite their throat. If I couldn't follow the dogs, what with the horse, the dogs'd come back to me and then they'd take me to where the kangaroo was. I'd put the dead kangaroo in the cart and we'd go home. Dad used to skin them. We'd peg the skin out and when it was dry, we'd bundle a few up and send 'em down to Geraldton to sell them at the skin place. Lots of families there used to eat the meat and we did too. Dad used to take what we didn't use out into the bush next day and burn it.

I didn't get a chance to play when I was a kid – there was always work to be done, cleaning up and looking after the younger ones. I went to school in Yalgoo – we went from six or seven to fourteen then. There was only one school with one teacher for between forty and sixty kids. I didn't *mind* school, only I had to look after the younger kiddies, so I could never put me mind to it properly. I used to take the younger kiddies to school – one of 'em was about two and the baby was a few months old. I left the baby in the pram and the other one used to play in the playground that me father made for her. On the verandah it was, so she couldn't run away; I took a few toys for her. They had their lunch at dinner time, a couple of beer bottles of goat's milk (with a teat on top) for the baby, jam sandwiches for the two year old. That's what I think kept me back a bit at school; I've sort of taught meself a lot since I got married; I didn't get on so well at school. The teacher used to be real good, he'd help me all he could, he used to give me something like a little book to read at night after I got home. When the kids had gone to bed, I'd do me homework.

When I left school I worked at the hotel, waitin' on tables, race time. I could always get a job in Yalgoo. Then I worked in one of the stores. I helped in a house too: I was goin' to school at the time, they had a coupla kiddies. I used to do what work I could before going off to school and feed the kiddies. What I didn't do before I went to school, I'd do after school.

The big rush was over but the prospectors used to come into town. They were a bit wild and woolly, some of 'em. Their pants always seemed too long for 'em, they used to pull 'em up and tie a piece o' string around their knees, their bowyangs as they used to call 'em. They used to generally carry a bag on their back for their pack and a hat to keep them from the different weathers. They used to come into the butcher's shop and get meat and then go to the grocer's shop for their groceries. They used to stop at the hotel for a few days at a time, some of 'em would get on the booze. They'd come in to spend their gold. Oh yes, I seen a lot of gold. We used to go out and pick it up too and take it to the bank and sell it. I don't know how I could explain, but they used to have a dryblower and it was made on four legs and used to shake backwards and forwards and they'd put the dirt in the top and it used to go through little holes. They had a piece of corrugated iron, just a very small piece, on a leaning slope and they'd let it run down on there and under. They'd have another piece, and they'd put an old flannel shirt or a piece of old blanket or anything on that and they'd shake it. The dirt and the bits of gold used to go clear. And this piece of blanket they had on the bottom used to hold the gold. Either that or they'd get what they used to call a planum of dishes. They'd have a sort of grave around the bottom of it and they used to shake it and blow some of the dirt out through the mouth. And then they'd get the water and they'd keep swillin' it and spinnin' the dirt off the top of it and all the gold would go to the bottom of it and stop in the bottom and they'd keep washin' and washin' and the gold would be left in the dish all on its own. Then generally they'd grab an old billycan or somethink and just put it away, and after two or three days, they'd put it all in one lot and take it to the bank.

It was not like it is now. Then the prospectors seemed to trust everybody, in those days, no ill feeling. They were mostly all single chaps, there wasn't many with wives. Some of them was real old men, the majority of 'em. They used to sit down on the ground anywhere and talk to us kids. They used to say: 'Oh well, I'll see yer next week when I come in; yer can come 'ome and cook fer me.' That sort of thing. I used to enjoy a bit of fun with 'em. They used to think it was great because they used to be in the bush on their own. The only time they 'ad anybody to talk ter was when they come to town. They used to try to tease us. We'd sit down just as if it were our father.

The camel drivers used to walk for miles and miles with their team. You knew they were comin' because you could see this great cloud of dust comin' along the road. The camels used to cart all the wool into town. They'd take groceries or whatever they needed on the stations, backloading, they used to call it. They'd load the camel at a ramp; fifteen or sixteen camels would pull a great big wagon and the same with the donkeys. Very nice chaps, the drivers were, you never heard them swear, real homely people they were. After I got married, we had camels of our own, about sixteen. We let 'em go in the bush and if we wanted 'em, we'd go and catch 'em and fetch 'em home. Each family had their own camels. They had 'em branded, their own brand on 'em. We'd use 'em for just drivin' around, we used to go out in the bush for picnics and that. We'd generally put a coupla camels in a big buggy – we could take thirty on that and we'd go out in the bush for the day. Quieter than horses, the camels were. They could get nasty if you was nasty to them, but I never ever had no trouble. You could travel coupla hundred miles a day with 'em, they could go real fast. No cars then, only camels and horses. At one time the Afghans used to drive the camels, but then our men found the horses were too slow, so they started in with camels too. Otherwise the Afghans would 'ave got all the work and our men would 'ave got nothing, so they started to speed up a bit with the camels too.

There were plenty of blackfellers too, the natives, hundreds of 'em. You'd see 'em all strung along the road for two or three mile shifting camp or goin' to a corroboree or somethin'. The poor old women walkin' along behind with the dogs and goats, the men ridin' in a cart with the old horse. They used to come in to town for a billy of tea and bread and jam or anything anybody 'ad to spare. They had no money and they used to go the police station to get a ticket from the policeman and then they used to get their rations. They'd go only to the shop where they'd get tea, sugar and flour, tobacco and a box of matches. In that time, of course, the corroborees was sort of sacred to them – they wouldn't want the white people going to them. They wouldn't mind now. In those days, we'd treat the blackfellers as neighbours. They'd come in and sit down and tell us about what happened in the bush, they used to be quite interesting, some of them.

The kids used to go to the same school as we did. They was a lot harder to teach in those days than what they are now. All

they knew then was their own wild language. But they used to
learn, the teacher used to sit one of 'em alongside of us; we
used to show them what to do. We all mixed together, didn't
make any difference. They was like our brothers and sisters.
Up our country where I was, the people were all friendly
together, never even heard of a fight amongst the darkies
themselves in those days. Not like now, they're always fightin',
but in those days you never heard of a fight. They used to
make a great big fire, twenty or thirty of 'em sittin' around
talkin' and singin' in their own language.

We got to know quite a lot of 'em. One family, the
Camerons, used to be always at our place. They used to live
on the outskirts of town, but they dressed better than what the
others did. They used to work, drovin' up north. They could
afford to have a bit better than what the bush nigger had.

Did I tell you about old Fanny? Her and her man, as she
used to call him, they used to work for the policeman there.
He used to look after the horses and keep the yard clean and
she used to help with the housework. This woman Fanny, had
twin boys and the whole family used to take these kids for a
walk of a Sunday, and we used to go with her, gettin' these
bardies out of the roots of the trees. She used to dig 'em out
with a stick, about that round, then some of the kids used to
eat them. I never ever took on the bardie – I had a lot of the
bungarra though. Her man used to go out the opposite way of
what we went and it was nothing for him to come home with
three or four bungarra, already cooked. He used to cook 'em
in the bush, he used to take a piece of paper; he'd come home
with three pieces about that long. Tasted just like fish to eat.
You made a big fire and scooped the ashes away and lay the
food in and covered it with their ashes. That's how they
cooked most of their food, any birds like duck or anything.
They just put it in, feathers and all and when they reckon its
cooked, they take it out. Skin or feathers come off and just
leave the bare bird. No salt, they never go that far.

We was on the stock route. They drove the cattle down from
up north, through Yalgoo to Mullewa. Yes, there'd be five or

six hundred cattle in some mobs. They used to go round the outskirts of the town. The ground was clear, just little salt bushes sticking up, so we could always see a mob coming for miles. The drovers – about eight and ten of 'em – used to camp the cattle. They'd ride round and round the mob till they all laid down, and then when they all laid down, some of 'em would go and 'ave a sleep. They'd just take in turns, two of 'em would ride around and round them all night. The least noise, the cattle were up and gone. It would take them days to muster 'em together again. They'd call it a stampede – they'd go for miles, through fences and all.

Racetime was once every three or four years, those times. Knock a few posts in the ground and tie a coupla tarpaulin over them for a bit of shade – it was always pretty hot up there. People used to come from Mullewa and Mount Magnet, all over the place. Everybody used to go out, it was a great day. We used to sit on the fence, watching them go past. Some horses got fetched from Mullewa. The jockeys would come from all over in case they got a race.

Every year the railway used to put on a picnic with a free train to it. This day it was to a big river. They used to have runnin', playin', rounders and two's and three's. Kids used to have skippin', who could keep it up the longest. Everyone took cakes and stuff. We used to look forward to the picnic – everyone would get together. It was the same with everything around those times up there. At Easter and that, everyone would get together. Never heard of fights in those days; there was back bitin', but no fighting, everyone was friendly.

Then we moved down to Mullewa and I worked in the butcher's shop. I met me 'usband on that picnic. I knew him a couple of years before we got married. We used to go to the dances, play cards and dominoes at home. You weren't allowed to go out like they are now. I suppose we could have gone for a walk if we'd wanted to, but I was happy enough to stop at home, so was he. Then Mum and I had a little bit of a row – she reckoned I should have done more to help her than I did. I dunno what she meant. I used to hand all me money over to her – all me wages when I was working, 1s 6d it was. One time there was something on at the hotel and they needed a girl to do the washin' up and the vegetables and that sort of thing. I went there for the week and when the week was up, that Mrs Clark came out and said, 'You finish up tonight, Annie.' She gave me half a sovereign and I ran all the way home, I was that excited, gettin' half a sovereign after gettin' 1s 6d. I just gave it to Mum. If I needed a new dress she would get it, she would mostly buy the material and make it herself. She was a good dressmaker.

Anyway, Mum and I had a little bit of a row and she told me to get married. So I got married. I done all the cooking for it. I wore a white frock – there was no veils in those days. I was married at home, there was no church there then. The Catholic priest came up to Mullewa; later he started a church there. We had the breakfast at home. Then we moved into a railway house, the railway gave us a house. I was sixteen and he was eighteen. He used to work by putting coal in the engines, it was a dirty job. He used to generally wear a grey flannel shirt and black pants. He used to change every day, so I used to wash every day.

I wasn't told anythink about marriage and the husbands didn't know anything either. You just wanted to get married. You'd talk about different things and it all just seemed to come to you. I know right up till my first boy was born, I knew nothing. When he was born, I got the shock of my life. See, me mother had gone to Geraldton – that was our market town: she used to go down every fortnight. I used to go down and do the meals over at her place when she was away and then we'd go home at night. This morning, I got up and got the old man's breakfast and then I went with him when he went to work over to me mother's place. He used to have to pass there. And after I'd been there a while, I started to get these pains in me stomach as I thought. I was in the bedroom doin' somethin' and I felt this terrible bearin' down. So there was an old chamber pot under the bed, so I got that out and I was lettin' this water run away into this chamber. And the next thing, a baby was there, almost into the chamber. Mum had a big black box she used to keep a lot of clothes in. A flannel lined petticoat was the first thing I seen, so I pulled it out and I wrapped him in that.

Then Dad come home for dinner and he said, 'Where are yer?' I said, 'I'm here, you'd better go and get Mrs McDermott' (she was the woman that used to come in). He said 'Why, are yer crook?' I said, 'No, there's a boy here.'

The afterbirth hadn't come away, and of course I couldn't move because the baby was still attached. Mrs McDermott didn't come because she was down to Mount Magnet that day, so another woman came. She only just came and washed the baby.

When me mother come home that afternoon, of course she had to take over. Hubby never come home till the evening. When he found out what happened, he laughed like billy-oh. I said, 'Yes, yer can laugh, yer swine.' Oh, I wasn't sorry about it really, I s'pose; the only thing is, not knowin' anything, not knowin' what to expect. When I was first married, I didn't know what sex was all about. Me mother knew I was expectin' a baby, but she never told me anything. So when I first felt the movements, I said to hubby, 'My stomach's rollin' round and round.' I couldn't work it out. He said, 'I s'pose yer been eating' somethin' doesn't agree with yer.' So that's what I thought. It opened me eyes, that day the baby was born. I didn't know what it was, it had me beat.

Then I had one baby pretty well every two years. There was nothing to stop them; in fact, we didn't seem to worry about it in those days. You'd fall pregnant and you never took any notice of it; there was no such thing as pills or anything like that. There was nobody to ask; you'd ask doctors and they'd just tell you no. I've often thought, surely there must have been somethin' they could have given us. You had to battle everything out yourself in those days.

I had seventeen children in the end, nearly all I was on my own. Most of them was born when we lived in tents in the bush. I used to work right up to the last minute before the babies was born. I didn't have much pain, it didn't last long enough. I used to squat to have them – I worked that out for meself. I used to bath the babies after they was born, then get on with the washin'; I didn't go to bed.

One time hubby went up to the doctor next morning – I had the baby durin' the night – and he sez, 'The old lady's 'ad another baby. I want you to come down and 'ave a look at 'er. 'I'm not goin' down there,' 'e sez, 'she knows as much as I do; if she doesn't feel too good termorrer, let me know.'

Long after I was married, a doctor I got to know – I got very friendly with him and his wife – he called for me a few times to go out with him to deliver babies because there was a fever broke out in the maternity part of the hospital. That gave me more experience, he used to tell me a lot about it. This doctor told me that keepin' the baby on the breast for the two years would keep you, because he says while the baby is suckin' the breast, it keeps the womb up and you can't receive. I think that must have been right because it was two years between with each of mine. When this doctor was goin' back to England for further training, he gave me his doctor's book. He used it when people were sick; it told you what was wrong and what tablets you had, after that style. It used to show pictures of different parts of your leg or your arm or your neck. They'd have the skin laid back and it showed you the different muscles and sinews and veins in your neck. They were all coloured in, in different coloured ink so you could pick out where it was the trouble.

The flies used to get pretty bad certain times of the year. Everyone would have bung eyes. At one time there was no doctor, only the old minister used to come up once a month. He had trained to be a doctor and then when the time come he didn't take it on, he went as a minister. Well, if anybody was sick, he'd come off the train, come along and see them and tell 'em what was wrong. He always had some medicines to relieve them, and then they'd have to go into what they called the hospital at Mullewa. I seen it and it was just a tin shed. They didn't have no nurses in those days, just ordinary women doin' the work.

My husband was always acting the goat. I'd say 'What are you goin' to give me for Christmas?' And he'd say 'Another baby.' I'd say, 'That's very fine for you, you don't have to carry it.' He was always teasing. He didn't show no worry about having babies. I don't know about other people's hubbies. I can say this though: even though he left home in the end, he would never have a row. He never went anywhere without me neither: everywhere he went I used to go too. If I went to a dance, I'd take perhaps the two youngest. He'd stop home with the others and when it would be time for the dance to finish, he'd put the kettle on and come up to meet me. By the time we got home, the kettle was boiling and while I was putting the baby to bed, he'd make the cuppa tea. He used to help out. He didn't begrudge us nothing. He always brought his pay envelope home and put it on the table; he never asked what I did with it, as long as he got his smokes. He never drank. A lot of men used to drink and homes got broken up over the drink.

Families used to help each other out in the bush. Our neighbours, we'd share with them, and anything they had, they'd share with us. I don't know whether it was just that the the wages was so small, we used to help our neighbours to have a bit of extra. I used to have eighteen goats; we used to give the neighbours milk, rather than throw it out. The goats used to keep us in milk, meat and butter all year round. In between we'd have a kangaroo or rabbit for a change. When we used to go out shooting we used to have people ask us if we would give them kangaroo meat to help them along. We thought it was better to give it to them than burn it in the bush. Just the same with the vegetables if we had a lotta cabbage or lettuce coming on.

There was no pictures or anything in those times, but we used to make up groups. So many of us would go to one neighbours' one night for a game of cards. Another night we'd go to another one. We'd go out to a farm for a surprise party. We'd take all the eats with us.

At times now I'm lonelier than ever I was when I was up in the bush. It's funny, I'm a lot lonelier now than I was when I was fifty mile out from town and never seen a soul for months, only just our own family. Whether it was just the wild animals around that drew the attention, that I don't know. Now I never go into any of the other flats here, I just stop on me own, there's always arguments and rows. There's only one woman's flat I go in; otherwise I just stop by meself. No, I don't think I would change my early life any, I'm mostly satisfied with the way everything was planned out.

Betty by the Sea

The kindly sun has drained away
Her life, like suds on washing day,
And left her in this chair on the sands,
Clasping her flowers with laundered hands:
As though a storm of breeding-pains
And work and worry, which scoured her veins,
Had passed, she opens her tired eyes,
Like still seas, to vacant skies.

— *Ronald McCuaig*

Rolling the scrub for farming, Tammin, 1905

She was born in Victoria in 1896 and came to Western Australia as a baby. She has spent most of her life in the country districts of Western Australia, but in old age she came to the city to live in a state flat. Her life has been sad and punctuated by violent episodes in childhood and married life.

The report of the timbercutter's daughter provides a unique example of the phenomenon of the 'battered child' early in this century. Cruelty to children often went unnoticed in the late nineteenth and early twentieth centuries. It is perhaps significant that the scandals which most often pricked public conscience in Western Australia and other communities were those instances where persons other than the natural parents abused and neglected children. Often these celebrated cases hinged around the practice of baby 'farming', when poor mothers left their children in the paid care of other women. In one famous case in 1907, a Mrs Mitchell of Perth, was found guilty of causing the death of an infant. But her trial brought to light the deaths of forty babies placed in her care in the previous six years.

This, and similar scandals, led to the development of legislation for child protection and the initiation of private agencies and government departments aimed at ensuring the physical safety of children. Whilst this may have reduced the incidence of 'third party' abuse – the abuse of children by persons other than their natural parents, such as their foster parents – we know today that much maltreatment of children takes place within the relative secrecy of the family. This had largely gone unchecked until a new interest in the rights of the abused child commenced about fifteen years ago in western countries.

Tree-felling, using crosscut-saw at Karridale, 1911

The timbercutter's daughter discusses her past very rarely, as she finds her memories very painful. She asked to be interviewed, but her subsequent revelations cost her a great effort and were followed by mental distress. But she wants her record to be published, as a reminder of some unfavourable conditions under which some children were raised in times past. The report which follows concerns her early life and does not indicate the sense of humour and patience she reveals in dealing with her present life.

1896 was when I was born, in Trentham, Victoria. I can't remember where that is. We came over to West Australia – a shocking journey, a terrible boat trip. I don't remember that of course, I was only one year old. My father went to the country to the south-west, to a place called Karridale, a timber mill. He got a job on the saw in the Karridale Mill. My mother went and my eldest brother and three sisters and me. Karridale was my first memory. It was quite nice as a place to live, beautiful country and that; we loved it of course.

But our life changed. My mother died in childbirth when I was seven. The baby died too. I can remember it as if it were yesterday. That's a strange thing – you can remember what happened years ago better than what might have happened a year or two ago. I suppose I knew she was having a baby, we could tell. I was at home, she was in another room when the baby was born. Mrs Nevill was there, the nurse. She told us that our mother had died. We didn't go to the funeral. She was buried on September 17th, 1902 in the cemetery at Karridale. She was a beautiful woman and my elder sister was just like her. Before my mother died, she wouldn't allow my father to make our lives unpleasant. He was a dreadful man. We were sitting at the table one night and something didn't please him, so he just picked up his dinner plate and threw it.

After my mother died, he got a housekeeper. She was a dreadful woman, a terrible woman and of course he let her take command of everything and she turned terrible. She ill-treated us children something terrible. It suited him to let her take over.

She was dreadful. I think there must have been something wrong with the woman. She'd get up during the night and she'd come into our room. I remember I heard my sister, my eldest sister . . . I heard her screaming – and there was this creature – this housekeeper – flogging her with a whip. She woke her up from her sleep. She wanted to be cruel to someone – she'd do it quite often. I think she was mad, she seemed to get pleasure out of doing unkind things. When we had a bath in the morning, she took a delight in filling the bath up three parts and holding us under, under the cold water.

We didn't know what it was to sit down at a table for a meal. She used to send us into the wash-house in the backyard. Bread and golden syrup, something like that. We never actually went without food – she didn't actually starve us – but we didn't actually have nourishing food. Everytime I go to the hairdressers, even now, they always ask me what this scar is on my head. She came in with the broom and split my head open and she had to take me to the doctor to get it stitched. She put out some story to the doctor. I was locked in my room for a fortnight and my father didn't even ask where I was.

She made my father take my eldest brother into the back room and flog him for nothing at all. She used to burn my brother, too, with a poker. It wasn't as if we were naughty kids. There was quite a big hill close to where we were living and we used to go up there from early morning and come home late at night. We were chopping trees down, just little children – chopping down trees for the fire. While this was going on my father did nothing. He was working – of course he knew – he never bothered to find out why was it we had these burns.

And as the years passed, this woman had a husband living at North Fremantle. They had a home at North Fremantle and she took us all there. And oh, she was the *cruellest* woman

that I think I could ever – Oh, she ill-treated the children
something terrible *and he never said a word.* So time went on
and time went on – she was a dreadful woman in every way.

My youngest brother – he's dead now – never used to sleep
in a bedroom; he had to sleep out on the verandah *no matter
what weather.* One of the neighbours reported it to the police
and they came and questioned all the kiddies and arrested
her. They put my brother, the one who was worst ill-treated,
on a pillow, to take him away; he was that thin and ill-treated.
Oh, she was a dreadful woman.

We never thought we'd get away from it until that morning
that Mrs Quick – she lived next door – called the police. I'm
quite sure the neighbours knew for a long time. No one
offered to help. They didn't want to interfere too much.

We went to the Salvation Army Home. They were wonderful
people, they still are. We were taken away each day to give
evidence in court. I remember going into the witness box to
give evidence. I can still see the judges, sitting there with wigs
on and that Dickie Haynes – he was recognized as *the* solicitor
– he asked me one question and then went right back and
tried to trick you. I must have been about ten or eleven. My
father got a great showing up in the paper but he wasn't
charged. She got two years' hard labour. She should have got
a lot more than that. You look back at what she is and you
think she only got two years. It was too light.

We were at the Salvation Army for a couple of years. After
the court case, my father rented a house and he wanted us to
live with him. He got my sister to keep house and look after
things. I can't remember much about this; it didn't last long. I
went to work for Jewish people, just housework – the ironing
and the washing. I've forgotten how long it lasted. My sister
Bonnie – she's still alive, living in Adelaide – and I both
worked. We got 5s a week and he used to take that from us.

He used to take *everything,* I'll never forgive him. I can't
remember anything about my father and I don't want to. He's
like a lot of men today, even today – when their wives go,
they go on with other women. After we left him, I never,

never recognized him; I never went to his funeral or anything.

When I was working with this lady – the Jewish family – and my brother was working in the country, he wrote down and asked me would I go up there. Near Pingelly. Of course I went up. He was working on a farm. He was lonely and he wanted someone close to him and that's where I met my doom! Six months after I went to the country I was married. I was just twenty, he was a farmer. He took advantage of me, that's how I got pregnant. That was not then like it was now: I was on my own and I wasn't experienced and I didn't recognize my father.

I was keeping company with a boy, a beaut boy, who was manager of the markets in Perth. And of course when I went up there and got myself pregnant . . . He wanted to marry. Forget it, he said; he still wanted to marry me. And I said no I couldn't. He said he was going to stay single, in the hope that one day I would be free to marry him. I felt although I was in love with this boy, I should marry the baby's father. And it's a strange thing, this boy stopped single. He died just a few weeks after the baby, who then became my eldest son, was killed in the second war.

What happened was, of course I got married and lived on the farm. It was very, very hard in those years, at the end of the war. Washing out under a tree in a kerosene tin. He had his own farm, with the assistance of the bank, but he used to milk other people's cows and loan out chooks. We had to clear the land. Oh, goodness me, it was all axe-work in those days, no bulldozers. I used to work with the axe until I couldn't do it any longer. I'd go out every day, even when I was pregnant. Women worked very hard, of course, then. When I look around now and see women who've got every convenience of every kind and think of the way women used to work hard on the farm, I often think what they owe to those women. Now they have everything to their fingertips.

I looked after the garden too. We had to keep the gardens in water. Water was a dreadful problem. You had to cart water from a soak, cart it to the tank. I used to do the washing under a tree in two kerosene tins: a fire in the open, a line between two trees. The house was just a room with walls of canvas. Our furniture was packing cases. You remember the big cases that you'd buy kerosene cans in? – that was my furniture. My kitchen table was made out of bush tins – I tell you it would open the eyes of some of the women now if they could have went up and seen it. But there was always enough to eat. We always had fresh meat killed and there were the vegetables. As the years passed, it improved very much and we ended up with quite a good farm.

The only thing I got out of my married life was my four children. They were outstanding. My husband was a bad-tempered man and he was a jealous man. When we were farming, if any neighbour came to ask him anything, naturally of course, I'd ask them to stop and wait till he came home and I'd give them a cup of tea. And after they'd gone, he'd accuse me of being unfaithful and that's one thing I can say: never, never again did I allow any other man to take advantage of me. It did pass through my mind once or twice to leave him, but I thought too much of the children. I never gave him a thought – it was the children. I was strict with them; they were good kids and everyone liked them. I had a lot of good friends.

There's a lot of things the children don't know, but I'm going to tell them soon. I had a terrible nervous breakdown. Oh yes, they had to bring me down to Perth to a specialist. When my daughter was a baby, they just caught me in time. I was throwing the baby into the dam, I was going to drown her. She was about ten months old. My nerves affected me in the head; I was depressed. In the latter part of my life (I've never told my family this) I found out he was going on with a woman who went over east. He went out one day and said, 'There's a letter here for you.' I opened it and it was from her. She cursed him and called him for everything. Next day I didn't feel like getting up, but I did and I called him and found him dead. He'd taken an overdose of sleeping tablets.

You see, she wrote the letter to me because when he'd gone

for this trip over east, he was supposed to have stopped with his brother, but he must have stopped with her and evidently, he must have been a nuisance. And I was going to put the letter in the fire so he couldn't see it, but he did and of course that was the end.

I wouldn't go through my marriage again for anything. Thank goodness for the kids. None of them take after him. I'm going to tell them about the accident, they've got an idea there's something happened. I never mention his name. If his name is mentioned, I get up and go out of the room. The doctor has still got me on nerve tablets. I had treatment and the treatment helped me. But I had to fight it too. I used to put a bandage round my head. My head used to throb that much – I used to feel that the insides were coming out. I still get dreadful nights. I suppose you could say I've had nerves all my life to a certain extent.

When first I left Old England's shore,
Such yarns as we were told,
As how folks in Australia,
Could pick up lumps of gold . . .

Goldfields folksong
— Anon.

Workroom in a lace factory, Midlands, England, 1890

The Factory Worker's Daughter 6

One impact of the Industrial Revolution in England was to open up avenues of employment to women outside the home. Thus, in the industrial north of the country, women have worked in factories for many generations. But in the colonies, where there were no large secondary industries, there was more resistance to women joining the ranks of factory workers. Of course, employment in factories may well have reduced even further the pool of women prepared to undertake domestic service. But it was also considered to interfere with woman's primary duty towards home life. The Inspector-General for the Insane in Victoria in 1907 associated the rising number of women employed in factories with the decline of the birth rate and the increase in the number of the insane. He said:

I view with considerable apprehension the steady rise in the number of female factory employees, and the consequent deterioration of that best of all institutions – home life, the interference with the training of housewives, and, in spite of the most perfect of factory legislation, the manufacture of bodily diseases in the younger employees, unfitting them to fulfill their highest obligation to the State, viz., Motherhood.

Born in 1899 the daughter of the factory worker went to work in a cotton factory herself, in Leicester, England in 1914. Her account conveys how a family coped with poverty. Other records of the time indicate that being poor was monotonous and dreary, but families who were poor were often independent, resourceful and hardworking. Given the trials of life, it is little wonder that the factory worker succumbed to the propaganda about emigration and decided to bring the family to Australia.

71

Nearly sixty years later, the factory worker's daughter who became a factory worker herself is a merry, vivacious eighty-one-year-old woman. She lives with her husband in a modern flat and she is an active worker in the local club for senior citizens. She sings in the church choir and plays bowls. Sociable and active, she recalls her origins dispassionately.

We were all so poor. My father worked in a shoe factory and was only earning 12s 6d a week wages and my mother had to pay 5s 6d a week rent. And eight children to keep on it, so it was a case of get out as soon as you could. I turned fourteen on the Saturday and started work on the Monday.

I was born in Leicester in 1899. I was the fourth. In the house, there was what we used to call the front room which would be the sitting-room. You come out of there into a little square passage, into the dining-room and then you'd go down into another long passage into the kitchen, where you'd do the washing as well. Then upstairs, there was my mother's bedroom and the boys' bedroom and then there was a little room that was over the front porch, so you can tell how wide it was. Mother just managed to get a double bed in it and there was five of us girls had to sleep in the one bed! Three up the top and two at the bottom! Which makes me smile, when you think now, how a person, if they've got four children, they've got to have four bedrooms! Really the times were so different – people just don't know how you ever managed.

I mean, bathrooms were a thing unknown, in those days. We just washed in the kitchen – the kitchen was a fair size. You'd have a big table in the kitchen, the copper'd be in the corner, the mangle on this side, and then perhaps you'd have a little table, there, where you washed. No showers in those days! And Friday nights came along and my mother used to have a big tub and she'd put that on the kitchen table and we'd all have a bath in that.

My mother was strict, very strict. She was a religious woman, although before she was married she was on the stage, a dancer. She had beautiful legs, dressed in tights. But by the time I was eight or nine, she was very strict. I don't really know why she turned so religious – she tried every church but the Catholic Church and the Church of England. Spiritualism, everything!

Sunday school! Yes, oh, we went three times on Sunday. Early in the morning, come home and have your dinner; afternoon Sunday school, come home and perhaps go for a little walk; back to church at night. And we used to have a fair walk to go to it. We don't do that on Sunday today and they didn't do it here as much as they did in England.

My mother made us kneel down before we went to school: we all were lined up and had to say a little prayer. I never could say it, yet I've always had the religious touch with me.

If there was an evangelist come to one of the halls or the churches, we all had to go along. He'd stand up after he'd said what he'd got to say, 'Now who wants to be saved?' Well, I think I was saved about four times! Every time he came we had to go up to the front to be saved. The Band of Hope, too, we went there once a week. It was just a little meeting, there was more children there then. They never had any enjoyment at it; from what I remember of it, someone got up on a platform and talked about strong drink. But you faithfully went along, where now, you couldn't get the kids to do it because there wouldn't be enough to attract them.

My father worked in a shoe factory. The wages they got – twelve and six a week! Mum used to go and clean houses – those big houses, as we thought them – she would go and scrub the floors. That's how she kept us going. Where there was a young girl in the house she would bring clothes home for us from there. And there was always the pawnshops around. We never did, but all our neighbours, on Monday, you'd see them with a big rolled up parcel and they'd take off their husband's suit and get them home again on Friday. Well, they'd get threepence for that and they'd have to pay threepence halfpenny to take them back. That halfpenny was interest on their threepence. It's just fantastic to think how things have altered, from that day to this.

Dad didn't talk about his job. In fact you didn't seem to have much to do with your parents, really. Not like the families of today, the kids are around you all the time. As soon as our meals were over, well, we went out. We never went anywhere else. We were never allowed to come in to listen to any talk. You played outside all the time until it was night, or till you were ready for bed. We never worried our mothers as far as I can remember, we just didn't.

After school, we'd march in and Mum would have a pile of bread and margarine on the table, and perhaps rhubarb jam (which I hated) or treacle. We'd have two rounds of that and then out we went again. Never thought of coming back and asking for any more! And if we were hungry (which I can't remember whether we were), we'd go into the park and eat little green leaves which we'd call bread and cheese. I'd say it was nature that took us there. No one would ever tell we could eat it, we just knew. But to ask for more than the two rounds of bread, you never thought about it. You never thought of asking either – we'd have got a smack in the face!

Tea would be about half past four. We never had any supper; it would still be two rounds of bread for our breakfast. No change. You never knew an egg – I had an egg every birthday. But I can't say we were really hungry – that two rounds of bread must have satisfied us.

In the middle of the day, we had a hot meal. We were so poor, Mum would go and buy a cow's udder for our meat which would cost perhaps sixpence. I can see it now on the middle of the table – it's like a big round yellow blob. Today you wouldn't eat it. She'd boil it and we'd have potatoes and then she'd go and get mangel-wurzel – they were like big swedes, they were really for the cows. Then she'd go up the lane and pick stinging nettles, that would be our cabbage. See, all cost nothing! That's how we had to live. To buy jam, you'd take an old cup and go to the corner shop and get a penn'orth of jam. You'd get a big cupful for a penny. Corner shops everywhere. You just went in – and often do a little pinch, too. I wouldn't do it, but I knew that there were others who would – biscuits would be in a box and they'd have their hand in there.

Wash-days, Mum used to have the dolly pegs in a big, wooden tub. Wash-days, every Monday I'd have to come home from school and while she was getting the dinner, we'd turn the dolly pegs. They're like four pegs and a round piece and the handle at the top, to wash the clothes and then she'd put them in the copper.

On Tuesday, Mum would go to a church meeting. Not every week, but school holidays. That was a gala day if we could go, as we had a bun and a cup of tea – it would cost a halfpenny. In those days, enjoyment, they never looked for it. In fact looking back, you wonder what they did. My mother used to make rugs. I imagine she used to do it as a relaxation after tea, but that sort of thing is rather vague to me.

Toys? No. But we appreciated what we got. Today at Christmas they hang a pillowslip up, but we hanged a stocking up – the foot would be stuffed with paper. Then there'd be an orange, if you were lucky, an apple anyway, and a few lollies, and a pair of winter gloves; there might be a little doll about so big. But you thought you were made to have got that! We did have a doll's pram, I can't think how we got it – we did have an uncle who'd come to visit us and I remember looking for him to come because we knew we'd get something, even if it was only twopence between us. He could be the one who would buy a doll's pram; it wouldn't be my mother who would buy it. Of a Friday night, we used to have a shopping night and used to love to go to the Penny Bazaar with him, as we knew he'd buy us something.

Our houses were semi-detached houses – that person's backyard would look into our kitchen. If you came out to hang clothes, they might have a talk with each other. I often saw my mother have a gossip. My mother had a neighbour next door that had cancer, I'd be about twelve I suppose.

She'd go in every morning and dress the wound for the woman, she had it in her stomach. It was one of those cancers that evidently broke out and it was like a tomato to look at. The husband used to go up the lane, and get bluebells and violet leaves and boil them every morning and give her the juice of them. Evidently he'd been told that was a cure, but it had gone too far. She died. You see, you couldn't afford doctors either and there was no such thing as home nurses then.

Now we had an old lady living next to us, our front doors were here and there. She'd sit at night time with a jug of ale and bread and cheese and she'd sit there every night. Yet I don't ever remember sitting talking to her. To us, she was a very old woman, yet she may not have been as old as I am now! When my grandmother was sixty, she used to sit in a chair with a shawl around her shoulders and she was an old, old woman, as far as I was concerned. When she went to church, she had a beaded cape on and a bonnet tied under her chin. She sat rocking herself in the chair. In those days, women lived for their homes and when the time was come that the family was out of the way, they just sat down and waited till life was finished. No, I wouldn't say old people were really revered; in fact, they were often more or less in the road.

My grandmother lived with us in the same house. Oh! – I was telling you, there was only the three rooms upstairs. Well, down the passage was another little room; she had that to herself. Every night, we used to have to fetch her a ha'penny worth of chips. We'd stand around, she'd bite the end of her chips and we'd wait for it! She wouldn't eat the top part and wouldn't eat the bottom part. When she'd finished with the chips, we'd have what was left over. This might sound funny to you, but every night we used to have to look in her head. In those days you had a lot of crawlies in your hair. Mum used to get kerosene and sulphur and rub that into our heads. Everyone had them but some people would have them more than others. Actually, my grandmother never had anything in her head, but she used to get us to look and she'd say, 'I'll give you a ha'penny for every one you catch.' We'd stand there for hours waiting to see if we could catch one, but we never did.

My mother was terrified of the workhouse. In my mother's time, the old people had to go to the workhouse and they had to scrub floors and got very little to eat. Mum was ninety-two when she died and she was here in Australia, but she used to say 'Don't you ever put me into a home, I don't want to go to the workhouse.' We tried to explain to her that the homes of today weren't like that, but she wouldn't have it. She had that in her mind that she didn't want to go to the workhouse. No, they were terrible days, they were. In my grandmother's day, had she not had anybody, she would have to have gone to the workhouse. They were prisons, and if they didn't do as they were told, I think they used to use the whip on them. So old people weren't looked up to in those days. I don't know how my mother kept my grandmother, being so poor. She may have got a little bit from the government, but I don't think so. Now that Mum's dead, there's a lot of questions I'd like to ask her.

I left school the day I was fourteen and went to the factory. They put me onto this big table, sorting out shoe laces, and getting the right ones together; we used to have to tie them together and put papers on them. But I wasn't there long before I was moved – I can't remember that part – but the next factory seemed to be something to do with corsets: it's something I don't want to remember because I was so frightened. The noise was terrible, it was clanging away, up and down all the time. You couldn't hear anyone speak for the noise. Then I went to the Coates cotton factory; I was to learn to keep the spools going – you had to see this line of spools was kept going all the time, they worked down from the top.

There was one part – I can't remember what I was doing – but there was a certain amount of waste you were meant to have – and this part isn't quite clear to me – and if you didn't have the waste you had to pay for it. But that's not quite clear to me.

I don't think I was very good at it, as they kept shifting me around. They only gave you a day to watch what was doing and then they put you on a machine of your own. You were so worried, it would start here and stop there, you'd try to get this one going – oh, it was all a nightmare to me.

No, I don't think it was strict, if you did your work properly. But they only gave you so long to learn. If you didn't do it properly . . . The boss used to sit at the end of the table: he was a nice old chap, head of these machines – I know I did get growled out. I seemed to be working there quite a while, but it wasn't that long.

It must have been my mother who wanted to come to Australia in the first place. In those days they were trying to boost Australia. Therefore, we'd go to these meetings and that would make you get the urge. Then they'd bring pamphlets around for you, how much it would cost you to go. So that's how it started. All these talks on Australia – they told you they picked gold up in the street. People came to better themselves.

Of course you might know that sixty years ago, Australia was all empty land, really, there wasn't the houses. At the lectures, they was always showing us orange groves and I imagined that we'd have a tent pitched in the middle of these orange groves!

What a ship we came out on! It was a cattle ship, turned into an immigrant ship. Thirteen times it broke down on the water. The steward used to come around of a night time and say: 'Well Mrs M, I shouldn't take your clothes off, tonight – the ship may go down!' Cockroaches everywhere. You can imagine what a cattleship was like – made for cattle. Rats and what have you! We had cabins – the lot of us girls, Mum and one boy in the one cabin: we had to sleep end to end, just the same.

But when we got here, it was pretty well a depression time. But you take England, coalminers out on strike, standing in line for a loaf of bread.

My father and one brother had gone out ahead a year before. But my father was a man who could titivate up anything and he had this house in South Fremantle done out quite nicely for us. We only had camp stretchers, but I was really relieved to find we hadn't got to be in a tent in an orange grove when we got here!

First of all, my father was working in a wine saloon in Fremantle for some Spaniards and after that, he went to be an orderly in the hospital. When he went there, his life was finished; he was a gentle man and he didn't like it. In those days, the first war – it was more crude, too. They'd saw a leg off and he'd have to wrap it up and take it to the incinerator. That turned his stomach – he died of cancer, I don't know if that had anything to do with it, I often think it did.

My father was a different type of man to my mother, being a woman – she had the stronger personality. She was one of these, well, 'you-were-in-the-job-and-that-was-it'. I had a sneaking regard for my father, more than I did for my mother. I suppose he had a softer nature. Where my mother wouldn't (and perhaps couldn't, but she never would) give us a farthing, my father, if he had tuppence in his pocket, he'd give it to us. I can only remember my mother buying me one present in my life; I never got anything out of my mother. I didn't look for it and I didn't get it. I don't know, I was the blacksheep or something. She did have a set on me. These last few years, I feel more hurt than I did then.

I got a job at a biscuit factory, earning 5s a week. Out of that I got threepence a week. When I started at Mills and Wares it was a very poor place, they were only feeling their feet if you can understand. There'd be perhaps a month at a time we'd have to be put off because there was no work. Well, my mother would say 'You'll have to get into a job straightaway', so I had to go into service until the factory opened again. I loved the factory.

When I started I was on creaming bags. We had to cream the biscuits. You remember cream fingers and shortbread creams? They were all done by bags. The cream was mixed up in another room and we had all these rubber bags and tubes and then they were laid on a belt, all these biscuits, and we used to stand by with our hands and squeeze so much on.

It's all done by machinery now – to see this machinery
dropping it all on the biscuits!

I never had the job, but a lot of my friends had to take the
biscuits off the trays as soon as they were taken out of the
oven. Well, they'd be standing there – from 8 o'clock in the
morning until 12 – and they'd be taking these hot biscuits off
the tray and all their fingers would be bleeding because they
were so tender. Their fingers were raw, red raw at the top, but
you see they had to get used to that too. For those few days
you had to stick at it, until your fingers began to harden to the
heat. There was no wrapping your fingers up – you wouldn't
do it. We didn't think anything of it. The conditions were
crude, that's all you can say. There was no sitting down. You
could go off to the toilet and we used to take a few of those
breaks. We'd have to keep our eye on the bosses of course, to
see they weren't around. We were frightened of the bosses –
they weren't too bad, I suppose. They didn't bother about
unions in those days. If there had have been a union, I don't
think they'd have been allowed to put us off when they did.
As soon as they got slack, the whole factory would be empty
waiting for the good times to come around again.

In between, people wanted maids. Off I'd have to go, but I
didn't like it. I didn't like the idea of having to work for
anybody, yet I didn't have the position to be stuck up or
anything. I could do anyone's housework and get praised for
it, and yet when they said, 'You sit in the kitchen and have
your meals', you felt you were beneath them. Maids were
maids. And yet we were never brought up to be too proud to
do it; I don't know what was in me that caused that but I
didn't like it. So as soon as the factory was asking for girls
again, I'd go back. I liked the company of the girls and it was
a different atmosphere altogether to working for someone.
With girls all round, you could talk – only if the boss wasn't
there. He'd sometimes walk in and say to the forewoman,
'Keep those girls at it', but apart from that, as soon as he
walked out we were talking again.

I'd say there was about twenty girls in each room; one was a creaming room, one was a packing room, and there was one where the girls had to put them in the tins. Today the machines do that, it's marvellous how it's grown and the different things that's in the factory that there wasn't in those days. Machinery, laboratories testing all the flour. It's an eye-opener to see making of the biscuits today. But I wouldn't say they tasted as nice! I didn't think I liked the biscuits quite as much.

In those days you had to stick at the one job. But now they'd be on this table one week and they'd move them onto something else the next week. Now the girl next door, she's Irish; she started at the factory and she said she didn't like it because they moved them from one table to the other. Now I should think that would be a very good idea, because nothing's more monotonous standing in one place and doing the same thing.

I went over the factory the other day. After sixty years; it's lovely to work in now – if I was younger I'd still go back there. I saw more the other day than I ever did when I was working there because once you're in the factory you just stuck at your job.

I was married from there as a matter of fact, in 1923. Mr Mills called me in one Saturday morning and gave me a three-tiered cake and half a dozen knives which I'm still using now. I was one of the forewomen – I'd got that far and then I was only earning £1 7s 6d a week.

My husband's family, when he was going with me, he said, 'Oh, she works in a factory.' They looked down on it, why I don't know. I've often heard since they thought anybody was rough who worked in a factory. But that wasn't so. Why I don't know – whether it was Australians wasn't used to factories – after all everyone worked in a factory where I came from.

I was twenty-three when I got married, at the factory on and off for nine years, head over girls for that department. Each department had to have a head over the girls which they called your forewoman. We used to have more fun with me being forewoman; I wouldn't say I made a good forewoman, I wasn't strict enough. Then we saw the boss was coming and that made a difference.

In those days, we lived inside four walls. I remember one of the times I had to go out to service and this girl used to take me home of a night-time, to her place, the evenings that we had off. You'd see them all sitting around, doing their crocheting. There'd be no wireless or anything. But that was their happy household, sitting around doing that! That was the life you led then.

When I was about twenty-one or two, I remember my mother slapped me on the face. My sister-in-law's brother and I, for some reason, walked up together from the bottom of the street to my gate. And out she came and smacked my face! Because at the time I wasn't inside. It must have been 10 o'clock at night and she thought it was a strange boy. She got a shock when I said it was Charlie Hicks! But I mean you'd have no life of your own. You'd got to be in by 10 o'clock and if you were allowed to sit in the front room with your boyfriend, the light had to be on!

I'd like you to have seen the glory box I had in those days. You'd say to the girls at work, 'Oh, come round and look at my glory box!' I had two pillowshams that I tried to work (I'm no sewer), a pair of sheets, two pair of towels, one night-gown and perhaps a few little round doilies. And that's about all – I was *ashamed* of it because I had no money to buy anything.

I was engaged about twelve months before we got married and it would be about twelve months before that that I *really* went with him. Life was different then – the men had to do the courting, whereas today, I reckon the women do the courting, they marry the boys. In our time, well, you just waited until you were asked. That's the only thing that's different – people used to do things they shouldn't do, just the same then as you do now.

Girls got into trouble just the same. But they'd be turned out of home, half the time. That would be the biggest disgrace. For instance, our neighbour worked at a boot factory and she was one of these people . . . a busybody . . . and as

soon as ever she knew that a girl was getting married, she'd
put down the date so she could find out if they *had* to get
married!

Our outlook now is better – we were very narrow-minded in
those days. A lot of people I knew of my age got married and
didn't know what was going to happen when they were
married. This girl lived with us, her parents went to the
country. In the bedroom, there'd be a couple of my sisters
sleeping over there, and her and I were in bed (you'd all sleep
together, practically, there just wasn't the room). I remember
we lay talking and she said something about 'somebody told
me what people did when they were married.' I said, 'I don't
care who does anything like that, but my mother and father
never did, they *wouldn't* do that!' She said, 'Mabel, you've never
been on a farm, but have you never noticed the animals?'
And this was how it was explained to me. My mother never
told me a thing.

You went with a boy and you knew you were getting
married and were quite looking forward to it, but you never
thought of anything else. You never even knew where babies
came from. It made many a nervous breakdown. It was taboo.
It must have been a terrible shock, the night of the wedding,
to find out what had got to happen. We didn't know what we
were getting married for!

There was one instance I've often repeated. We were
working with a girl, at the factory, that was going out with all
sorts of men, if you can understand. Oh! It was nothing for
her. We, at the time, said, 'Well, I don't know how you get
these men. How could they fall for you?' She said, 'Well,
come out with me sometime; you'll soon get somebody.' And
blow me, she brought two boys along. This girl who was living
with me, of course her people were as strict as my mother
was. So off we went, we thought we were going to have a good
time. And they took us down to the beach . . . and the next
thing, of course, they wanted something, and I believe she had
to get her hatpin out for *her* chap! And I kept saying 'No! No!
No!' and he said, 'What did you come out for, then?'
Anyway, afterwards I heard that this chap had been noted to

take girls' pants off. So I was darn lucky to get away from him!
But you see, that's all that girl was going with them for. But,
in our ignorance, we didn't know; we just thought we'd like to
go out with a boy, and that was that. I'll never forget that, and
of course people always said, 'You were mighty lucky to get
away from him.' We got home like two scared rabbits!

You wouldn't be allowed to go out with a boy unless he was
brought home first, to be examined by the family, too.
Where's now, the girls are allowed to go with any Tom, Dick
and Harry. But it makes you wonder if things are overdone
now. When I look at girls today, you have nothing to look
forward to. You used to look forward to a wedding, or getting
engaged to a boy, but not now. I'd rather have had *my* time
than today. We felt there was something in life for us. There's
not now, and I think that's what's wrong with the world.

I've been back to England twice. I didn't want to stay.
They're so packed in there. And of course, there's the first,
second and third class too, there. The lower class, the middle
class and the upper. Well, we were lucky if we ever got in
touch with the *middle* class. I don't think there's that here in
Australia in the same way – we all seemed to be the same.

Of course, in England being young, I didn't have much to
do with the upper class. Now the house my mother cleaned,
to me, it was a mansion. Beautiful big rooms and the bay
windows. Anyhow, when I went back to England, I thought
we'd go and look at these big houses that my mother used to
clean. And I was disgusted. As a matter of fact the black
people were living in them. I thought they were mansions
when I was a kid. But there was nothing to them.

We were looking for bed and breakfast at the time. I
remember going into the corner shop and I said to the chap,
'Can you tell us where we can find bed and breakfast?' He
said, 'Oh no, not round here.' I said 'What about those places
over there?' He said, 'Oh no, the blacks all live in there.' I
said, 'Fancy that!' And that's where my mother used to clean
those houses!

A woman named Phyllis came into the shop. The chap said,

'Phyllis, would you know anyone with bed and breakfast around here?' She stuttered: 'Nnno but IIIII . . . 've got a room, if you'd lllllike to have a lllook at it.' I went to look at the room – we were glad to go anywhere. It was a dark, dingy place, reeking with cigarette smoke, 12s 6d a night. I said to my husband outside, 'Doesn't look too good. It looks as if mother died in the bed and she never made it!' When you sat on the chair, it was damp and you'd swear the cobwebs went from the floor to the chair! The place smelt of scent, getting rid of the other smells! When I turned the bedclothes down, the dust rose and hit me in the face. I hated sleeping in that bed – I could imagine the woman dying in the bed. We didn't stop there more than two nights. In fact, I was going to stop in Leicester a fortnight, but those two nights did me – I was disgusted with the place. You look through a child's eyes far differently to when you're grown up.

I was really made out for factories, but I wouldn't like my time over again at fourteen. I'd really like to have been a lady! No, what I'd like would have been to go onto a farm, to go into a farmhouse and work. We used to go with my grandmother to a farmhouse and get the milk. To see this beautiful kitchen with all scrubbed tables, you'd see the maids with their white aprons on. Oh, it looked lovely. To go into a place like that with other maids might have been different to service, I mightn't have felt they were looking down on me. But I never got the chance, it was just factory or nothing.

Water for sale, goldfields, 1895

Laying the water pipeline from Perth to Kalgoorlie, about 1900

Why Women Rule the Men

In days of old, as we've been told
The women ruled the men
The men, like fools, did make new rules
And ruled them back again.
But womenkind were not content
They wanted the franchise,
The world is topsy turvy now
And that is no surprise.

Some females in the labour cause
Have got great intellect
They have a system of their own
And that is most perfect.
But take all women, good and bad,
There is this much about them
To keep this world as it is
We cannot do without them.

— *'Percy the Poet'*

She was born in 1893 as one of a large family; she was brought up on the goldfields and she had a limited convent education. She went into service; she became a union organizer and then, in 1920, became the first paid woman trades union secretary in Australia.

Clearly, that appointment indicates that this woman was unusual. Yet, the background she describes was similar to that of many families living on the goldfields at the time.

After school, the brewery worker's daughter went to Perth and then into service. There was very little protection for young girls against exploitation by their employers: servants were lonely, they worked long hours, their living conditions – food and accommodation – were poor. The main aim of most servants was to get away from the demeaning drudgery of the task. Of course, not *every* servant was exploited – or rather, not every servant viewed herself as exploited, as the account of the odd jobber's daughter suggests.

In old age, the brewery worker's daughter is lively, concerned and warm hearted. Once briefly married, she divorced her husband and now lives alone and enjoys the peace of her small flat. She keeps in touch with the 'girls' she worked with through the Depression and before, and is in close contact with her nieces and nephews and their families. Her reputation as a fiery, severe leader is tempered by a well-judged sense of humour, compassion and bright twinkling eyes.

✻

When I was four years old we came to Western Australia from Adelaide. My father worked in a factory in Adelaide and he had to get up at 3 or 4 o'clock in the morning to feed the horses. He tried to form a union and they sacked him, and he couldn't get a job in South Australia. So that's why we left Adelaide.

My mother came from Ireland. She came with a lot of Irish girls in a big ship, she said. I don't know how big the ship was – probably nearly as big as this room! The girls all had bags with them to pick up the gold that you could pick up in the streets and take back to Ireland. They had to get these Irish girls out here to populate; the men were here but there were no women you see. Those days, the passage was paid – it didn't cost them anything. All they had to do was come here and populate the country – which they did! I don't know how many descendants of my mother there are!

The girls were brought into Adelaide. Everything was very primitive then, about the 1850s and 1860s I think. It must be very hard for you, or people today to visualize the time when there was *nothing*.

She worked in a hotel, such as they were in those days. And she got married in South Australia to my father. He always said he was a mongrel, really. He was half English and half Irish. His father was actually a 'Sheehy' – we weren't convicts or anything – but when my grandfather came to Australia, there were notices everywhere where there was work, 'No Irish Need Apply'. So grandfather changed his name to 'Shelley' which was a English name.

My grandfather was an engineer – a well-educated man and my father was born in Australia. I remember he said that when he was going for the Irish girl that an Irishman said 'Damn colonial! The cheek of him, going for an Irish girl!' That's how I know Dad was born in Australia; we never asked him, we weren't interested!

When you're young, you only think of yourself and for years, I thought my father was a terrible man. Now, looking back, I think how absurd that was.

My father had nine kids to keep and he worked in a brewery where you can smell beer every day of the week. And he never drank a drop. I think that's great: he had to bring home his pay, £3 a week. Now and again, he would break out, but it's a wonder he didn't break out more often – there was nothing to look forward to. Those days there was nothing – no entertainments, no books, no music, no anything, you just lived from day to day.

My father knew about history and he'd tell us about it and he'd talk about books. He was a kindly man. And he never lifted his hand to us, any one of us. It was left to my mother to do that. But he brought his pay home every week.

He was Catholic but he wasn't a church man, he didn't believe in that nonsense. (I don't believe in it either, just quietly!) Once I believed all the nonsense I was told, and poor old Mum did keep it up for the children's sake – we all had to go to Mass. When we were grown up, we dwindled away, like everyone else.

Looking back, my mother was strict. She wasn't one of those mothers who was always mothering you. Those Irish girls were very strict in those days; they ruled the roost quietly and you never heard 'damn' in our place at all. We were only working people, but you never heard a swear word. And I never heard anyone say, 'You mustn't'. We just didn't.

But I think my parents must have had a happy marriage. All this talk about the word 'sex' these days – then we didn't know what it meant. But I was only saying the other day, they must have had a very good sex life, my father and mother. They had nine kids. They got on well together and there was nothing else besides. There was no going out because there was nothing to go to. It was all they had. If sex was repugnant or anything, the marriage mightn't have lasted.

When we left Adelaide in 1897, we went to Esperance, right on the south coast. I was four, so I don't know why we went to Esperance, but we lived in a house on the beach and we played in the white sand. Then, of course, the goldfields began and Dad and one of his friends went overland in a big dray with a big white horse to Kalgoorlie. Everyone was going

to Kalgoorlie, making their fortune. Dad sent us first, he had
to put us on the ship. We were just handed up the side of the
ship and everybody on the ship was sick, except me and the
Captain! At Albany we caught the train to the goldfields.
Everyone was talking about this large family of children on the
train and somebody bought us a canvas bag of water. I can see
all the men running up and down and admiring the family in
the carriage. But Mum still had to pay fares, so when the man
came round to collect the money, I was put in the lavatory! I
was sore about that, as I'd wanted him to see my new dress!

We got to the goldfields, looking down at the red earth! I
don't remember our first house, but I remember where we
lived eventually. It was one of the three best houses in
Boulder. Iron, in the main street, four rooms – I don't know
how we packed in. No front verandah, but a back verandah.
Everybody else was in hessian.

In Boulder, Dad must have realized he was not going to
make a fortune, as he was never a miner. First, he started a
business, quite a good business, an aerated water business,
quite a big place. We must have had the business for some
time, because my brothers used to go to the factory and work
there after school. Then the business broke up and he had to
find work. In a brewery. My father was a man who couldn't
have a drink of beer and forget about it. He had to leave it
alone because he had to go the whole thing, see. He just had
to keep on drinking until he was under the table. So, as I said,
he didn't touch it all the time he worked there, even with the
smell.

In Boulder, in those days, we children were kept strictly
indoors. The town was packed with people, rampant with
men. We'd be sent out, quite dressed up, but we had to stick
together! No one could move out of the group – there were
seven girls! The miners were very generous; when they saw
children, they threw money to them. But we weren't allowed
to even look sideways. I hoped when the money came that I
could pick it up! I suppose my mother was worried, but most
of the miners were law-abiding, decent people in those days.

A lot of them were single men, and came from all over the world – they were from everywhere. And on a Saturday night! I remember a bloke named Callahan standing on the corner of the street. Everybody knew him and he was a toff, dressed up in a good suit, collar and tie. I think he may have been a fighter.

I never heard the word 'prostitute' and I wouldn't know what a prostitute was. I remember when my sister, Ida, became a young lady. You weren't ever supposed to show your ankles and we dressed in flowered hats and long skirts with trails on them. And high necks with bones in them. And you walked along, lifting your trail. I remember my sister putting powder on – no paint – and my mother went stone mad. It's the first time I heard the term 'Bad woman'. Only bad women did that – a shocking thing! But I didn't know what a bad woman was. I was quite ignorant and I never heard the word 'sex' those days. 'Sex' meant male or female – I was about the greenest thing ever on the goldfields! When you're reared up strictly like we were and you keep kids down, you resent it without knowing it. So when we reached sixteen we pleased ourselves!

My mother had seven girls so she had to make our clothes. She bought a Singer Sewing Machine from a man who came round – 2s 6d a week – and she loved her machine. She was pretty busy, cooking, buying wholesale at the market, doing those horrible tubs of washing, boiling the copper outside in the yard. At that stage, we all wore starched clothes and ironed the clothes with those awful heavy irons.

When we went to the goldfields, there was no water. We used to have to buy water, condensed water, 2s 6d a kerosene tin and when you bought it, it was hot. We always had water to drink, but I don't remember too many baths. The tub was put in the bedroom and we were all given a bath out of the same water. At school there was a bucket of water for us to have a drink out of.

In the winter time, the rains filled great tanks in the backyard and mother had a beautiful vegetable garden. My sister and I had to go into the bush to get water from a soak of some kind, and we'd bring the water home in tubs. But when the water supply came through in 1903, it was a different matter. Everyone had gardens overnight, almost. People would wave to each other as they turned a tap on.

One Christmas, before the water came through in the pipes, there was no water and we couldn't get any. We had no water to cook Christmas dinner and it had to be bought at Mrs Conway's boarding house. But what really bothered me was our goat. My mother poured *lemonade* into a tin and gave it to the *goat*. I remember that because I felt I would have liked the lemonade.

School was prayers, prayers, prayers, morning noon and night. Kids today in the first class know more than I did when I left. I left school when I was fourteen. My sister, Ida, and Mum left the goldfields and came to Perth. Mum wanted to get away from the mines, so that my brothers didn't go to work on the mines. She was fearful of that – men were getting killed like flies down the mines. Oh, it was crude! All at once there'd be a whistle blown and you'd know there was an accident. A lot of men were killed on the mines and besides that, they were getting miners' silicosis and that. She was determined her boys would never go down the mines and they didn't.

I got a job in a boarding house in Boulder as a kitchen maid. I was always a good little worker and a bit of a character too. I used to wash up the dishes, peel the potatoes, scrub the floor. I was busy – not too busy – but I enjoyed it there. There were boarding houses all over the place, all sorts of women running them. The landlady was a big fat woman, nice looking; she was getting married to one of the boarders and the other boarders were quite cross about it because she was giving the best to him, and she was giggling like a girl all the time.

When I came to Perth, I was about fourteen, or fifteen, or sixteen. I worked all the time. First in a house in Havelock Street, some Jewish people where I was a maid of all work.

But I was too much of a rebel; I'd do a fair day's work, but they couldn't make me do any more. The woman liked me, because I was a darn good little cook. But she was horribly mean. I lived on bread and honey. I had to help with dinner parties, so that was nutritious occasionally. You had enough work to do, cooking three meals a day, as well as washing up and keeping her kitchen clean. I had a little room and I had a candle in it. I used to get a dish in my bedroom and wash myself – I wasn't allowed to use the bathroom. No days off. You were stuck there, there was no such thing as going out anywhere.

When I gave notice to this woman she was wild! She decided she'd do spring cleaning, but she was so angry that she went around and I was carrying the stuff for her and she was doing all the work and I was smiling to myself! Then she tried to get me to scrub the kitchen floor, so I said it wasn't the day for scrubbing it. I could have done it but you know how some people get you on the wrong side . . . so I wouldn't scrub it and she wouldn't pay me my wages. I told her off: I said, 'I hope the next girl you get, Mrs So and So, that you feed her on something else but bread and honey.' And then I went to a young lawyer in Perth. (He was Irish and he came from the goldfields so my mother thought he was marvellous – anybody Irish was always marvellous!) And of course this lawyer had no time for servants, particularly those who gave their bosses cheek. He snapped at me and said, 'Who told you you could leave the job?' I said, 'She did.' So he had to write her this letter, telling her to pay my wages. I'll never forget her reaction: 'Get back into the kitchen where you belong,' she shouted. So that was my first Perth job.

The man of this house later became a parliamentarian. Once a colleague, an MP, rang and I answered the telephone. 'Is Miss Catherine there? Or Master James?' (They were the children of the house, but I'd never go for this 'Miss' or 'Master' stuff.) He found out there was only me in the house and invited himself over. What a terrible cheek! I might have been an orphan girl without any self-respect who needed

affection and who had fallen for his line! The orphanages of
those days were full of girls who'd be sent out to service and
they'd come back pregnant, to keep the orphanage going!

Then I worked in a boarding house. What a place! The
room I slept in was crawling with cockroaches. I'd get up at
6 o'clock in the morning and work until eight at night. Once
at 8 o'clock after working for fourteen hours she said, 'Now
you can do the ironing!'

I used to have a half day off: it was heavenly to have a little
bit of time to yourself. And to be free. Sometimes you might
change your job, just to get a day off. When you were leaving
a job, you never regretted it, because you had nothing to lose.
You'd get something as bad, or perhaps worse, or a little bit
better, perhaps. And you'd have a lovely day off in the
meantime, sitting in the park or going home to see the family.

Then I went to the United Hotel. Hotel was better than
working in private domestic, because you'd get three good
meals a day and a clean bed; you see, publicans always gave
you good food. I didn't have any money, those days, because
I was helping a sister of mine. You didn't worry about that
those days. Three meals and a bed and if someone wanted a
quid off you, you gave it to them. So I didn't have any money
when I got this sore throat. The housekeeper said 'You must
get your throat fixed, Cecilia.' So I went to the doctor who put
me in hospital overnight and it cost me £5 and I didn't have
the money. And the housekeeper said, 'I'll give it to you,
Cecilia.' And she gave it to me, so you can see she wasn't a
bad sort.

When I was leaving this job, I was desperate. I had no
money. And this dear little man used to come from the
nor'west and they said: 'What a pity. He always gives us a
pound when he's going!' A pound! So I said 'Tell him I'm
leaving, will you?' Nobody did. So I said 'I'm leaving tonight',
I said desperately. And the dear old man put his hand in his
pocket and gave me a quid – saved my life. You couldn't ask
your family, they didn't have any money, no one I knew had
any money. Wages were low and you went from job to job.

Then I went to work at the Beach Hotel. I looked through
the window at the sea and thought 'I wonder if I'll ever cross
that sea?' But wages were so stinking low, so I didn't think I
ever would. The woman who ran the hotel was erratic. She
was very careful with me. I was a nice looking kid and
therefore in the dining room; they've got to have a nice
looking waitress who's not falling all over the place. So she was
careful with me, but hard on other staff, men and women,
and I was getting sick of this. Staff would walk all the way to
the hotel and she'd send them off with no money in their
pockets. Now the woman who owned the hotel picked those
who couldn't answer back. This Pommy housemaid said to
me: 'Look I want to stay here! I know it's terrible, but you do
get a few tips, summertime. I want to save money.'

In the dining-room one day, they had Lady Somebody or
Other and some Society People. When she picked on the
Pommy housemaid who couldn't answer back, I answered for
her. I got angry and put on a turn. I did it deliberately, I can't
stay angry for long. I called her, and her two-bit place for
everything: I threw glasses and smashed them. And the
manageress was saying, 'Cecilia, Cecilia!' She was worried that
Society would hear. Here I was doing it all for the housemaid
and I didn't even want the damn job! So that's how I left
there.

I went to another damn place, tea rooms. It was a broken-
hearted place because the war was on and everyday,
somebody's boyfriend or brother was killed. It was grim.
Twenty-two and sixpence we got; we bought our own
uniforms. I had a room in Perth, no breakfast and I couldn't
afford a cup of tea. When you got to work, you'd look around
for a crust of bread and sometimes we'd steal a cup of tea and
nearly choke when the manager would come down and catch
us drinking it! Then at lunch-time, we had a meal for a girl –
two bits of meat with gravy around it, and a potato and
sometimes a green. That was our dinner and nothing at night-
time. Then one day, Lil (she lived at home, so she could live
better than I did – anyone living at home could get a feed at

night there), Lil said, 'We're going to stop at eleven for a cup of tea, will you join us?' 'Oh yes,' I said, 'I'll be in it, Lil.' So at 11 o'clock, Lil got a cup of tea ready. We stood there trembling from head to foot and had this cup of tea and a piece of bread and butter. And the boss came down to see what was going on. We were expecting him to explode, but he wasn't a bad old sort and he didn't. And, for ever after, we did have a cup of tea at 11 o'clock. We were starved! And sometimes we'd be working up there until midnight; we used to run through the streets in our uniform to catch the last train. No overtime, not even heard of.

There was a union of kinds, but the secretary was a timid person who was frightened of everybody and couldn't prosecute. During the war, he joined the conscription side and his wife joined the Khaki Army. They were women dressed in Khaki and they were out recruiting. Those days there was no free entertainment on, so the best entertainment was to go to listen to these khaki-clad women. They used to take meetings and the crowd followed the noise. These women were talking: 'Our husbands are away at the Front and we are here tonight, to get someone to take their place.' So the crowd laughed – they were a joke.

The first war was only a trade war anyway. Our lives were changed by the first war, it was all so sad. I was broken-hearted about it. I remember saying, 'Why were people going to kill each other?' I'd never heard of this before. Trainloads of men from Boulder went to it and never came back. It was a terrible thing and a fiasco. They were sent to the slaughter and slaughtered by thousands. They were made to go in to be killed like animals.

I used to think, what did it matter to us if someone shot the archduke of somebody or other? But politically, I knew nothing at the time. I was only grief-stricken because people I knew were dying. Dear little Bobby was only eighteen; his people were in Meekatharra, he had nobody in Perth. I wasn't his girlfriend but I knew his family. So Bobby went off to the war and wrote me a pitiful letter telling me how dreadful it was in the mud and slush with people lying dead all around him. He was killed and his mother never smiled again.

I was always interested in politics. Dad and Mum were Laborites and wherever I went at work, I seemed to be taking somebody's part. I used to collect for the Russian Revolution. I'd only read a couple of books about it when it was announced in the evening paper in 1917 that it had happened. I walked on air that the people had revolted.

After the war, I found myself in North Perth helping with the Federal election but there were still problems at work. My father said, 'You girls should go to a union meeting.' At that stage Labor was in the doldrums and the Trades Hall was as dead as a dodo. I went to see the Trades Hall and the game was on! I seemed to have horse sense. I supported a group of girls at a meeting and whenever I moved anything after that, it was carried. After that, there was a dispute and the Trades Hall called a stop-work meeting. Come the morning, no one turned up. So I rushed around the town like a general saying, 'Out, out, all out!' They dropped their buckets, fell over their mops and swarmed from everywhere and the strike was on. It was 'Miss Shelley' from that day on and my life changed. Everywhere I went, people knew me and there was publicity. The papers started treating the disputes committee with respect, because they were fighting back.

Then I was nominated as an organizer of the union and was elected. I went around and people joined up in droves – I knew what victimization meant. Then I went to Kalgoorlie to address a strike and after I came back, the union secretary was sacked and I was elected a Union Secretary. No, I wasn't surprised, I wasn't surprised at anything in those days!

Most of us in the family lived to be quite old. But I'm very glad I haven't got any children and grandchildren. 'I've got to go and see Gran,' they say. They've *got* to! I feel very *lucky* about that. I've seen people in hospital wishing the old person would die and be done with it, because they *have* to be there. It's a dreadful feeling to have to have about somebody you've loved, that finally you're sick to death of them.

As a matter of fact, I have a sister living now. She's living, well in a way, she's living – in one of those homes for old people. I get horrified about this business for myself. I told the doctor one day. 'Look, I'm not afraid of dying,' I said. 'Everybody dies.' But I am afraid and horrified about the half-death. Darling, I never want to be in one of those places; I just couldn't bear it. My sister and her husband died in a private hospital which was supposed to be a very smart place. But honestly, it was like a prison – lights out at 8 o'clock. Some of them were very sick people, but my sister wasn't at first and at 8 o'clock she had to go to bed. Bath-night was Thursday night and that was it. They gave them one decent meal in the middle of the day. But at night-time! – it was tinned spaghetti rings, or nothing, or a tiny bit of meat and a scrap of lettuce. Old people would have to be hungry on that basis, it's profiteering. And when my sister was dying, she was in a room with three others and she didn't even have a screen around her. And you'd go in and sit there on the chair and they hadn't even emptied the pots underneath! You could smell it while you were sitting there and it would be there for hours and hours. And that was supposed to be a good place! Mind you, I know there *are* some good places. You can't condemn them all. And compared to what they call the olden days when there was no nothing for anybody, things are better. There's a club now for retired women in every corner.

Most old people go into these places because there's nowhere else to go. I can't *imagine* anyone going in by choice! They all sit around a room looking at each other, they don't even talk to each other. My sister sits up there like a zombie. Five o'clock at night, they fill them up with pills and they are zombies for the rest of the day. And the old men have to sit on the woodheap, there is nowhere else to sit. There are chairs on the verandah, but they are never used when I am there, the old men sit outside.

I'm sure old people worry about this. A friend came yesterday, a lovely person, retired now; she lives in one of those homes. I said, 'I've got a horror of a place like that.' She said, 'My dear, we all have.'

Mary Jones is her name
Single is her station
Happy be the man
To make the alteration

— Anon.

An arrangement of wildflowers (kangaroo
paw and others), photographed in 1911

A visit to the antipodes during the early nineteenth century must have been as fascinating for the European natural scientist as a late twentieth-century trip to the moon is for our contemporaries. A number of scientific expeditions visited the shores of Australia in the late 1800s and early 1900s and specimens of exotic flora and fauna were caught, classified and collected. Amongst those particularly interested in the Great South Land were the French, who sent at least five officially sponsored scientific expeditions to the southern and western coasts of Australia before 1820. Knowing of their presence, the colonists of Sydney became restive. Anxious to prevent a possible French presence on the southern coastline, they sent off ships to claim the territory. The only settlement to have survived from this is Albany.

When the odd jobber arrived by steamship in 1886 in Albany, his daughter was a babe in arms. But her parents would have seen a magnificent natural harbour of striking beauty. The straggly little town set on the hilly coast was then the major port for the Colony of Western Australia. Most sea traffic called at Albany on its way to Melbourne or Sydney or on return to England. The passengers were disgorged at the port, took a bumpy week-long journey by dray to the capital, Perth, some five hundred kilometres away. Lady Brassey, whose ship called at Albany in 1897, had to stay aboard ship as there was no suitable accommodation in the town for an English gentlewoman. She reported that the town of Albany was very under-developed – it was practically impossible to get fresh fruit and vegetables, for instance.

The odd jobber set out to try to remedy this deficiency. Most of the childhood of his daughter is associated with the growing and selling of food. The daughter still lives in Albany. Now in her mid-nineties, she has lived in the same cottage for fifty years. It is in a deteriorated state, with ricketty, unsafe verandahs covered with tangled vines. She is now frail and her sight is impaired. She feels very vulnerable in the house on her own – heartless boys have broken in – so she sleeps next door at the neighbour's. But she is adamant that she will not enter an old people's home. She is gentle and soft spoken, with a fey manner and clouds of loosely pinned white hair.

My memory is not so good now, not as good as it was five or six years ago. I can't remember a lot of names, the names of the bush flowers. In fact I've put my own names to them – pincushion, creeping vine, rich green, things like that. Pincushions come up near a soak or something. There are pink and white, and yellow ones in some cases.

I'm in my ninety-fourth year. I was born in 1885 and I arrived here in Albany in 1886. They were advertising in England to get suitable people to do things on the railways and my father came out. I don't know what part he was to play. He was used to working as a gardener on those big estates in England and at one point he was working in the coal mines. He was one of these that liked to know how to do lots of different things. He did that throughout his life. He got on really good, he never was rich but we were comfortable.

We came out to Australia on a steamship – it was the second little steamship that was built. It was only small and they couldn't fit very much of our furniture on. It had to be all taken to pieces and the curtains wound round and then stacked on. We had a terrible rough trip out to Australia and father was sick nearly all the way. The ship put in at Albany and they put him off to pick up; it took him a while. And, of course, he had to start work that he didn't understand much.

We managed to get rooms for a while. They wanted to settle Albany, to make it a settling place so as they wouldn't lose it;

the English crown you see. They got out as many people as they could. I remember the soldiers that came and I remember seeing them on parade on Strawberry Hill, in their red jackets and caps and they had trousers with blue stripes on the legs.

My father started chopping down trees to make a bit of a shack. You should have seen the great big trees – they were that much in girth. Then we had to wait for things. There was a French family living not far from us and he was building a house for his family. He had quite a family and they had to get windows and doors out from England. That took months. He came running along one day and he said, 'Look, my wife and I have decided to let you have this window for your house, so as you'll have one comfortable room and we'll manage with some boards till you can get another from England.' Wasn't that lovely? We had no locks or anything in those days, just boards across the doors so anyone could walk inside. We were scared of the native people, even though they were very nice to *us*.

Father used to go out working, chopping down trees. Wood had to be sawn up and that was hard work, there was nothing electric. You put in hours at a stretch like that and you had to watch what way that tree would fall. Father was good with cattle too. There was plenty of work, but we didn't get much pay. All that father got for the family for himself, my mother, myself was 17s per week. That was to get your bread and everything. Father put a few little potatoes and things like that in his pocket when we came out from England and they grew.

My mother always was clean and she was very particular with her washing and that. I've failed her these last few years, I can't keep anything now like she kept it. She was always busy. She got up early and got breakfast for father, because he used to work down by the lake. Then she started on the fowls. We managed to get a few eggs from them and sell them and mother always seen to the fowls. Oh, she used to help in the garden and she did our baking in a camp oven – there was no stove – and she used to make all our bread in it with fire underneath it, outside. The camp oven was iron and everything was cooked in that really. The joints and the vegetables, we had a few vegetables. And then we used to catch a few things because we had to make do – we only got meat once a month when we were lucky, because it was only when a farmer killed something we got beef. You could get mutton but you had to make a sauce for it; put with the vegetables it was very nice. (And, you know, I still have mutton shanks, it's lovely, I think.)

Father used to catch wallabies and possums, but they were horrible, you couldn't eat them – too strong, they lived off the wild bush. But we used to have a lot of animals. I used to skin them and we'd cook the entrails for the pigs and the fowls. Bandicoots, too. We used to have them for breakfast – the cats used to kill them, there was a lot about. Father used to take them from them and skin them and they used to taste just like fish.

Our relatives would send us flower seeds from England by the penny post, on the quiet. There was a lot of young blades in the town – young men who had their girls and it was the fashion on Saturdays always to take a bouquet to their best girl. We'd strip the garden sometimes, getting bouquets for them and we'd sell flowers from the house for sixpence and threepence. And then we got vines to grow and potatoes – I can see right up that highway now, sacks and sacks of potatoes, we were digging for them. We used to sell them, after keeping enough for us in the season. Cabbage, carrots, parsnips, cucumbers and tomatoes. Father thought it was lovely to grow tomatoes in the open (they're all grown in England in the greenhouse).

We used to grow watermelon – you could only carry two at a time, one in each bag to town to sell and they wouldn't cut them in those days, so it was a weighty trip to town. We used to sell them down at the port. The ships had to buy food for their passengers and father used to buy bananas and that for us.

The gold-mines had opened at Kalgoorlie so Mr Morgan and his family came down [to Albany] and I got a position there at his big house. He was a man with a considerable amount of money. He used to come to live in Albany at times. And the family were very kind to me, it was just like my own home there. I used to go home to my parents at night; only when Mr Morgan was away, then I slept in the room next to the lady. She was kindness itself to me. She had a maid, a lady's maid, who taught me how to pack cases and that and I found that very nice. I used to do anything they wanted done. I'd do a bit of cooking if that was wanted; they had a cook but she had a day off. What was I called? Oh, some would say, 'Oh, where's the kitchen help?', or some such – or sometimes I was the animal help. They had cages with birds in, that's how I got so fond of birds. Since then I've had them nearly all my life.

I had a very nice time at that house; I had nothing to complain about. They were very cultured people; they had a French lady's maid. I used to hear them say, 'Voulez-vous passer la moutarde', and I still remember some of it. There was a French sister at the convent, she said she would teach me French anytime. But father wasn't very well supplied with money then, so I had to let it pass. Oh well, it wouldn't have been much use to me really, although it would have helped when different boats was in Albany, down with some of the officers, . . . because different languages was spoken.

If I was in waiting on guests at the table I'd wear a dress in whatever colour they wanted, and wear a cap, just a bit of lace and a bit of embroidery. You didn't get the money they get now for twice the work done, of course, and they have proper hours now; they finish at certain times. It was long hours then – we used to work through until we finished our work, we got just the same pay. Most big houses kept a boy for sweeping the yard outside and bringing in the firewood; but sometimes I chopped the wood because father taught me from a youngster. And I've chopped wood all my life and never hurt myself until last month. I didn't mind helping with the cleaning, I used to do it at home. She always had the silver cleaned every Friday.

I had nothing to complain of. I had my time off – one afternoon a week and I could go to church on Sunday if I whizzed around in the morning. If I had to do the cooking that day, I'd go in the evening. I had to pump my fire up and put on coal if it was low, to help it stay alight while I was away. I never was away long. I used to very often go at night, then there was nothing to do in the house until after church time and I would be back for that. On my afternoons off, I generally went home, I'd walk home to see my parents. The family I worked for was very kind to me. They'd often go for a drive in the afternoon in the summer, they'd put me in the landau and give me a lift to the main road and then I'd walk down to where we lived.

I liked a quiet life. By the time you'd worked all day and evening, if you don't sleep in a place and you have to work at nights, you don't feel like going out too much after that. People used to often come to our place and have afternoon tea Sundays. We were friendly with people around.

I had boyfriends. I never married any of them, my father needed looking after. I knew several very nice gentlemen when I was a young woman. I did my embroidery and things like that and kept it away all those years, it's never been used. Now I look at it this way: none of these gentlemen had very long lives and I'd have been left on my own, a widow, with any one of them after four or five years. I've often thought that was the trouble.

My mother died after the first war and I stayed home to look after my father. I used to be so sorry for father, I stuck to him all those years. You see, in England, before I was born, father had two sons. A virus went right through London; there was a terrible lot of deaths and this virus, whatever it was, carried them off. One of the two boys was very clever and years after, father used to say to me that when he would wake up in the night, he could see the little man pulling the stool out and jumping up on it to say such and such a psalm. And I used to be so sorry for father. He was a nice, kind, gentle sort of person. I felt he was always so nice. I felt I had to replace the two little boys. Once I saved my money up and got him a very nice cow for Christmas.

Father told us we shouldn't do this or that, certain things which I'm very thankful for, because it doesn't worry me a bit and I haven't got into any trouble – I never did. He used to say I had to be honest, I must never take anything that didn't belong. If father picked up something that didn't belong, his first thing was to try to find out who it belonged to, because there was nobody that had anything spare in those days. So if anything was dropped on the track, it was an accident. So it was never ours, any of the family that picked it up, and everybody was asked if they owned it. We were brought up to help each other and I'm very thankful for that. I see such a difference in the younger people now. You see everybody scrambling around and ruining the earth.

I don't know that I'd change anything if I lived over again. I had a happy life, I loved people, and I loved the garden. I loved flowers, loved birds and animals. I've spent a long time with flowers and birds. I used to talk to them . . . I do even now.

Immigration

[Mr Jordan was sent to England by the Queensland Government in 1858, 1859, and 1860 to lecture on the advantages of immigration, and told the most extraordinary tales about the place.]

Now Jordan's land of promise is the burden of my song.
Perhaps you've heard him lecture, and blow about it strong;
To hear him talk you'd think it was a heaven upon earth,
But listen and I'll tell you now the plain unvarnished truth.

. . .

Here snakes and all vile reptiles crawl around you as you walk,
But these you never hear about in Mr Jordan's talk;
Mosquitoes, too, and sandflies, they will tease you all the night,
And until you get quite colonized you'll be a pretty sight.

. . .

To sum it up in few short words, the place is only fit
For those who were sent out here, for from this they cannot flit.
But any other men who come a living here to try
Will vegetate a little while, and then lie down and die.

– Anon.

Sunday afternoon by the river, England, about 1890

She has lived already for 101 years. When she was aged twenty-three, Queen Victoria died. When she was in middle life, the First World War started and she was old enough to draw a pension by the start of the Second World War.

Born in Bristol in 1879, the clerk's daughter lived in England for thirty-five years, and immigrated to Australia in 1914. Her perspective on the world might be described as late Victorian. Her values give priority to parental authority, to acceptance of death and fate, to betterment by emigration. For the English working class living in the cities, the Victorian era was a time of dense, overcrowded living, long hours of repetitive work in factories for uncertain return, Sunday escapes to the green fields and lanes of the country. All these features are reflected in her story.

The clerk's daughter was one of six children living in a house with one bedroom. Her schooling was terminated in 1892 when she was thirteen and she found a factory job to help support the younger children. She went to the factory on six days a week and on the seventh escaped to the pleasures of the country. Her courting was circumscribed by parental authority and a strict view of what stood for respectability. Respectability was very important to many Victorian working people. More significant than riches, it was achieved in part by not associating with folks seen to be lower in social standing, particularly not with 'rough' people. The clerk's daughter carried this attitude to Australia.

Although she lives in a hospital for old people, she is active and bright. She chirps away pleasantly to visitors and shows a remarkable skill for mental gymnastics about numbers. For example, on what dates do Fridays fall in 1982? At 101, the clerk's daughter has the immediate answer.

Today is very, very different, it's a different world today. But I was born in 1879 in Bristol. I was brought up in Bristol, so were me 'usband. There was six of us: I were the youngest but one. My father when I can remember was a traveller in the brewery, but he never travelled. No. He were there for seven years, then he did clerical work. He come from Worcestershire, he come from good family. He was well bred, my father, a very nice gentleman. Yes.

They don't tell you much in those days, not like they do now, not even their age, really. But my mother was a lady's maid; she had her own room and everything – she was waited on. She used to go to the castles, because she had to carry the jewels. She had beautiful 'air; she'd do it in plaits and put them over her head, you know; me father used to say she looked better than the lady she travelled with!

I was born very primitive, in comparison with today. We just didn't go anywhere much, you see. But I was always lively and I was always singin'! Father got a pianner, my brother played tin whistle and I could sing. I could sing all sorts of music and still can today.

I was good at cooking cakes and I made Christmas pudding, four eggs, at Christmas time. My father used to say, 'Now we'll try a little bit first on the pussy!' We were very fond of cats and my brother had a dog, too. When the Salvation Army come playing along the street, this dog would get up and sing and make an awful noise.

I remember going to school – we had slates in those days. I used to try to be there first, to give out the slates. I was wonderful at decimals. I wish I could have gone on: I didn't have to leave, but I did at thirteen and a half. I was in the 6th standard.

Then I ran around and found a place. I rang the bell. A

man come to the door. He sez, 'How old are you?' I sez, 'Thirteen and 'alf.' (I felt so indignant of being asked!) He said, 'Got your birth certificate?' I said, 'No, but I can soon get it,' and 'way I went, got that birth certificate and went back. I found a bucket and turned it upside town. There was a window, a long window and I looked in and saw they were making boxes. I thought, 'I'd like to do that,' so I went around to the door. The manager came and I said, 'I see they're making boxes in there. Would you employ me?' He said, 'Oh, no,' he said, 'We don't take learners.' So I went to another place for three months for nothing, to learn how to make boxes! Wedding cake boxes, with folds of white lace inside and silver edges of course, they don't have them now. Cigarette boxes, all kinds. Sometimes there was a gross wanted immediately. How much work you did was put down in a little book, so the slow ones was penalized – no unions, nothing like that at all. About a thousand girls.

I'd go at eight in the morning till six at night-time. One o'clock, we had our dinner. Didn't have morning tea and afternoon tea, like today. Five and a half days a week! The foreman was a lady, treated you well. I made two gross of boxes in a day – I was quick – for 3s.

I had to pay 6s a week board and I had to save a bit of it. The house we lived in was only 6s rent. There was six of us but there was only downstairs and a bedroom upstairs: it wasn't like big houses in Australia. You could put all the houses in England into a corner of Australia!

I must have been at the factory eight years or so, until I got married. When I was going with me 'usband, he were sixteen and I were nineteen. I had anaemia and the doctor said I were to have a bottle of Guinness stout each day, plenty of milk and to go in the country. So I had relations in a village in Gloucestershire. It were so nice there, lovely little lanes and all; me 'usband and I went and got mushrooms there on Sunday afternoon.

Courtin', we used to sit inside in the parlour – we had lamps and we'd turn them out, sit and talk in the dark in front

of the fire. Me mother would come in and light the lamp.
We'd do nothing wrong though!

One summer day, we went to Scarborough. It took eight
hours to go there on the train. I had a blue dress, and a
lemon coloured hat. It poured all day! We were there all day
and we didn't know where to go! So we sat in the station and
ate our food – we stayed there as long as we could.

And then we used to go sometimes on a Saturday to a tea
gardens, summer-time. We'd have strawberries and cream and
salad, and different things. Then we'd all go in the fields and
sing. We'd come back about 9 o'clock. They was our
pleasures, they were simple but I liked it. Very primitive, that
way.

You know the suspension bridge at Bristol? We spent our
courtin' up there. We used to sit up there and talk and talk
and talk. I weren't allowed to go out, only 2 nights a week and
I had to be in at nine. He had to be in at half past ten. He was
locked out one night, so he went up in the woods, stopped
there all night, and went to the office. His parents locked him
out again and that was a dreadful thing. His father put his box
outside during the night and turned him out. He kept his eyes
open and he found another job in Manchester and he sent his
photo and he got the job. He was up there eight months when
we got married. He used to come down and I went up once
and stayed where he was boarding. They was lovely people,
they were well-to-do; they had a business and a lovely house.
They had two daughters, but no son, so he was like a son. I
went up and got married from there. Nice wedding – two
white horses. I wore a grey frock made of chiffon. We was
only five in church. I was twenty-four.

My first baby was a girl; it was named after a dead baby, my
sister's baby that died, Ellen Violet. The next one was named
after a dead baby of me 'usband's mother, Oswald Francis. I
had two sons and a daughter and Ellen Violet, she's still alive,
she's seventy-four. She were born before the doctor came, I
didn't know what was going to happen and I were by myself.
We didn't talk about these things much.

In Manchester, I seen the Pankhurst girls, there was a shop around the corner where those girls used to buy matches. I found out they were some of these suffragettes. We didn't take much notice of them.

When Queen Victoria paid her last visit to Bristol, we went down to see her. My father was right close to her carriage: he said her cheeks were something awful; she looked like an old washer-woman. We couldn't get near her, we was on a bank with a couple of thousand children. That were the last time we seen her.

My husband's father had never been in a theatre in his life, they belonged to the Brethren. My husband took him, but it wasn't to be. The news came that Queen Victoria had died and they got their money back, and went home. You used to hear a lot about the royal people but you didn't see them very often. Now that Queen Alexandra, she had what you'd call the King's Eagle – her husband was very fast, don't you see? Edward VII was very fast and a lot of them were then. It used to come through to us; the news got around.

In Manchester, I used to go to the theatre a terrible lot. I used to love the plays – anything historical, *Richard III, The Merchant of Venice* who must have his pound of flesh. In Manchester there was fourteen theatres in one street! I used to like the comic opera; we used to go to all of them.

In 1911, we decided to come to Australia. Me husband had to get a new job. He went to London and got a recommendation and he opened a set of books at Whittakers, but he had to start at the bottom, so he thought we'd be better out here. He wanted to go to Canada, but we took my little boy along to the doctor. He had chest trouble. The doctor said, 'You don't want to take him to Canada! He needs the warm. The sooner you go to Australia, the better.'

My husband went to Australia three years before me. I come in 1914. I didn't know what to think about Australia, I didn't know what to expect. I didn't have a good impression of it. I thought it was overrun by blackfellers. 'Oh, I don't want to go *there*,' I said!

My husband met the ship in Fremantle; he came on board and I introduced him to the different ones that I'd been friendly with. Eight persons in one cabin. When I got off the ship and saw the port, I said, 'What a dirty old place!' Oh, the *mosquitoes* near the water! Oh, the *flies* and different kinds of *wasps!*

My husband got a home – everything in it. But I'd been there five months when he was transferred to the country, Goomalling. There was nothing up there – two grocershops, two banks, that's all. We come to this funny house – the bedroom had no door; there was just a partition, so you could jump up and see who was in bed!

In fact, I got to like Goomalling. I became friends with people and I didn't want to leave. Church, choir practice. But my husband spent most of his time up in the club. I used to go out with the doctor, they had pneumonic flu after the War. So I used to take out whisky and blankets. I remember we went out to one farm, where there was a baby: we had to take it to another farm because his parents couldn't look after it.

Never seen a blackfeller in me life till I came to Goomalling. They didn't interfere with me much. They used to come into town for their rations. They weren't really black people, just half-caste. Oh *no,* I never *talked* to them. And now there are blackfellers in Bristol! My granddaughter were there and said, 'You'd never know it now.'

My son went off to a farm when he was sixteen. He learned the farming, then he had to go to the War; my two sons went to the War. In Goomalling my 'usband done everything. He took timber round the place, taken orders, measured up houses, did everything; paid himself. Then I remember the Depression came and all the older men were put off. We were in Perth again, my 'usband was put off. Everybody in the building trade, bricklayers, carpenters were out. They were hard times, they were, but I got over it. Those times, my husband and I made the best of it. If you have nothing else, you do make the best of it.

I could be contented anywhere where the living was; I had

the children and I like it better where it's warm – I can stand
the warm better than the cold. But I still wish I hadn't had to
come to Australia. I got on all right, but I wish we stayed in
England. And I wish we could have managed to come to
Australia together. There's quite a few here in this home from
Bristol. I had a calendar last year and one man asked if he
could see it. There's another big man from Bristol, and one
from Fishponds, where I come from. And now, there's
another man, just been in here a fortnight!

When Father died, he 'ad nothing wrong with him, just
senile decay. I've got a feeling I'm going to be like that! I've
got to my age and had nothing wrong. Oh, I had pneumonia
last year, and the year before that, I got the flu on top of
bronchitis. I did think that was the end – we all did. But it
wasn't. I come good again, so they can't get rid of me! And
I've got a wonderful memory, it gets me into trouble!

The Roaring Days

Their shining Eldorado
Beneath the southern skies
Was day and night for ever
Before their eager eyes.
The brooding bush, awakened,
Was stirred in wild unrest,
And all the year a human stream
Went pouring to the West

Oh, who would paint a goldfield,
And paint the picture right,
As old Adventure saw it
In early morning's light?
The yellow mounds of mullock
With spots of red and white,
The scattered quartz that glistened
Like diamonds in the light:

The azure line of ridges,
The bush of darkest green
The little homes of calico
That dotted all the scene
The flat straw hats with ribands
That old engravings show
The dress that still reminds us
Of sailors, long ago.

— Henry Lawson

The grocer in front of his shop in Meekatharra, about 1910

Sixty-five years ago, she married an Englishman on the Western Australian goldfields. The couple journeyed to South Wales, where the grocer's daughter began a new life as the florist's wife. Now widowed and nearly ninety (she was born in 1891), she lives alone in a small, semi-detached house set on a precarious ridge, isolated by about sixty steep steps from the street. A bad chest and poor sight have confined her to the house for years – she is helped by neighbours, local shopkeepers and the council home help service. None of her three children live in Swansea.

As we have already seen, quite a number of women migrated from other parts of Australia to the Western Australian goldfields in the last years of the century. But overall, and in spite of the efforts of the British emigration societies, figures suggest that nearly as many women left Australia during this time as arrived. For example, from 1901 to 1910, 204 000 women arrived in Australia, while 175 000 left. This travelling of Australian women has not been thoroughly investigated and a study of the reasons for their departure would make fascinating reading. Presumably some, like the daughters of the grazier and the bishop, left for nostalgic, but temporary visits to the 'Mother Country'; others, such as the barmaid's daughter and the grocer's daughter, departed Australia's shores permanently.

We are inclined to think that mass travel was invented by Qantas and British Airways, but even the accounts of this book suggest that women were on the move between 1890 and 1918. What was different for many of these early travellers, though, was the aspect of *finality* of their journeys. The long sea journey to or from Australia was often the beginning of a process which could

The grocer's daughter, photographed in about 1912

not be reversed easily. Transplanting into a different society often meant losing touch with fundamental roots. In fact, it might be said that one mark of a successful transplant was when the emigrant viewed the soil from which she grew as infertile and unproductive.

The recall of those who move from one society to another is probably more faithful to the *actual* images perceived at the time by the Victorian child or young person, since such images remain uncontaminated by later events and unconfused by later developments that occurred in the same place. Much of the detail might vanish, but the outline of the image stays sharp. There is less of a temptation to reinterpret things which happened in the light of later experiences or changing social attitudes. For example, the attitude expressed by the grocer's daughter toward Aboriginal people is consistent with the view that many people held at the time, namely that Aborigines were scarcely human. This can be contrasted with the views of the farmer's daughter, who became a nurse in country areas, making it difficult to ascertain whether the impressions of a small girl were revised in the light of the wisdom of the adult professional.

In her girlhood, the grocer's daughter suffered losses which would be regarded by many experts today as potentially catastrophic. Her mother died when she was young and then her favourite aunt. She 'lost' the rest of her family by migrating to Wales. She experienced two major migrations in the first quarter of her life, but she accepted these and other experiences with an ease that some may view as supine. How she could achieve this without either looking back or breaking down is of interest, in view of today's notion that loss is a major cause of mental ill health.

My parents were proper Australians, my father was born in South Australia and my mother in Ballarat [Victoria]. There were five children and my father was a grocer. We decided to go West because my mother was ill and the doctor said a sea voyage might do her good. We had relations there, you know

125

– well, an uncle and aunt was there in a place called Mount Magnet, a mining town.

I should think I was about seven or eight. I remember coming over in the boat from the east to the west: we were the only children on the boat. The troops were goin' back from the South African war then; we had a good time with the soldiers.

We got to the West, to Fremantle you know, we stayed in Fremantle a while. Father went up on the 'fields then, about openin' a business. We stayed in Perth, at a big coffee palace somewhere in the main street, Hay Street they called it. And then we went up to Mount Magnet and stopped off, we didn't stay there long. Then we went up on to Cue and mother went to bed there that night. And she never got out of that bed for nine months. Until she died. So that was the end of her and she left all of us.

We had a nurse night and day: it nearly broke my father, all that expense – night and day for nine months. I knew she was very ill, but I never heard nothing about her going to hospital, we were only children and we took it as it was. Yes, there was a doctor used to come. It was a funny thing, my mother was ill really when we got to Cue. She went to bed that night and there was a knock at the door: somebody lookin' for somebody else. My father (I don't know how he sensed it) said: 'Are you a medical man?' He said, 'Yes.' So he called him in and he attended her that night and after that.

She died of cancer. I didn't know she had cancer, you know – it's only since I grew up that they said about it. When we asked what was wrong, they said she had sores inside. That's all I knew. The other children were too young to know – one was only eighteen months old and the other twelve months older. She was buried there; the cemetery is a long way out, but I can't remember that. But I remember that my father's brother was out in the bush and he took us children out to tell them that she'd died, I just remember that.

I was about nine when she died and I had a sister older, about fourteen. So of course, she kept house for a while and

then she married young – when she was eighteen – so I
carried on then. I was just a girl of fourteen and I left school
and I carried on. And there was my mother's sister over in the
eastern states and she was married, but she had no children.
So my father sent over to her and she came over. She lived
just close by us so she used to give a hand. I looked to her
just like a mother and bless me, then *she* died. So I was
unfortunate.

That was more shock to me than when my mother died,
because I depended on her so, you see and I was older. I
missed her terrible. I think it was cancer again, so they tell me.
It was rather sudden. I felt awful after that, more so than
when my mother died.

I was quite put out that my sister was marryin' and I had to
carry on. I said to my father, 'I'm going to get married when
I'm eighteen.' He said, 'All right, we'll see,' he said. But I
didn't mind leaving school, I didn't mind a bit. My father did
used to help me a lot; Sundays he'd help me do the cooking
and that. Had three of them going to school, you see: I'd cook
the meals, cut the sandwiches, do the washing. I carried on
like a wife would. My father was a great help though.

Cue was only one street, up one side and down the other.
His shop was in there, a fair way from the house. There was
no big mines in Cue, just Day Dawn out of the town. But I
had nobody on the mine. Most I knew were out in the bush
cuttin' timber, that sort of thing. By our house was bush and
they used to have camels passing by our house with the
Afghans cartin' stuff from the stations. They used to camp
near there. One of them, my father used to write letters for
him. So he used to call in and my father would write a letter
or read a letter for him, I don't know what about. We went to
an Afghan's Christmas once, my friend and I and a few
others; we had plenty of *fruit*! All the fruit came up from Perth
and usually it was half bad by the time it got there.

There was a Church of England and a Methodist and a
Catholic – there was three churches. My friend was Church of
England and we used to meet after Sunday School and go for

a walk. We went to the Methodist chapel and used to look
forward to it. When it was terribly hot, we used to hold service
outside. We had it 117[°F] in the shade.

We never used to do anything, just stay home. We used to
go to a few dances in Cue, my sister and I; my father used to
look after the children and we'd go every now and then. That
was the only bit of pleasure we had, I think and things goin'
on in the church, too – socials we used to look forward to.

We used to go to church (they call 'em churches out there
and call 'em chapels here) – Band of Hope and sign the
pledge and all that. And of course we stuck to it. We were all
teetotallers – I never tasted any of it. I've never tasted a drop
in my life, nor my 'usband.

There was two or three hotels just in the main street. Plenty
of drink there. They used to say of a Saturday night, they used
to take 'em out of the pubs, put 'em in a cart, take 'em down
the end of the road and tip 'em all out. Terrible drinking up
there, but we never went near it. Thirst, I suppose, it was so
hot, you see.

Not long before I was married, we were in the house and
we heard a terrible bang. We rushed out and there was a man
blown himself to pieces, not far away. Bits all hangin' from the
trees, picking up pieces all over the place. Never found out
what happened.

Down towards the town there used to be a row of houses. I
thought they were Chinese – a row of 'em down there – but
we never had nothin' to do with them. They had a little place
to themselves, you see. They used to walk about, but I never
heard no fuss with them, though.

There was a terrible lot of Aborigines. We used to get them
around the doors all the time. Bread, meat and tea – they was
the three things they asked for. We used to say, 'Go down the
yard and get a tin' (one of these big fruit tins, you know) 'and
I'll give you some tea.' So they used to bring up a tin out of
the rubbish, to give them tea. Used to say, 'Go and get a stick
and stir it.' They never washed or anything, they were dirty
really. If you give them clothes, they'd always put a woman's

skirt, you know , the placket hole over the shoulder, so it was up here one side and down the other. We used to give 'em clothes we didn't want: dress 'em up, you know. The women used to do all their carryin' and everythin', the men didn't do much. And the dogs – they used to go down the bottom of the yard if you'd give 'em food – and they'd sit around and give the dogs a bit.

But I never let 'em in the house, *never*. Some would let 'em in and they'd do washing and all for 'em. But I'd never let them in. Too dirty. Flies galore. I don't think they ever washed or anything. I was kneeling down doin' the stove once, bleachin' the stove and I got up and there was one behind me. I said, *'Get out of here.'* I said, *'Didn't I tell you you were not to come in the house.?'* Oh, she wanted to help me, she wanted to do some work . . . 'If you want something to do,' I said, 'you take the broom,' I said, 'and sweep the yard.' But she didn't understand anything I was saying and jabberin' away, off she went. They used to go off to the bush – you'd see their fires in the distance of a night. No, I wasn't frightened of them, I didn't think of fright. The government used to give 'em blankets in the winter time; they used to issue blankets once a year, I suppose to keep 'em warm. Then they were beggin' food around people, and tobacco they used to ask for.

The house was mostly this stamp-metal stuff and we had two rooms and then a big passage right through and the bedrooms was like canvas. There were no proper houses, they were not built like these houses! I remember we had a terrible dust storm once, and half the roof come off and parts of the house came down. Terrible dust storms – we used to call them willy-willies. Always lived alongside the railway. There used to be one train a week. People would crowd on the station to see the train comin' in – it was a red-letter day.

We went off to Meekatharra when I was fifteen, sixteen. (I know I had me hair down me back, tied with a bow.) My father went ahead to get the business and then I came with the children. From Cue to Nannine by train, then by coach.

I kept house until I was twenty-three. Oh, I was quite

happy. I only had what me father give me. Then when I got married, the two young sisters took over. I suppose me father knew I'd get married some day – he was very good. My sisters eventually married in time.

Meekatharra is where I met my husband, in the chapel there. They used to tease me about him, I don't know why. They'd say, 'There goes the little Pommy, Vi!' (He come from England, you see.)

The man used to go around readin' the water meters used to 'camp' with him. He told me one day, 'I'm going to bring the Pommie down to see you.' Then there was a bazaar in the chapel and they put him on the flower stall (because his people were all flowers here in Swansea) and me on the fruit. They was trying to get us together, I think. So we got together, anyhow. He was doin' assayin', on the mine, he was doin' that when we come away.

No, I don't know how he got to Australia, or why he decided to go up there. I remember he told me that he thought to go abroad (like they do now) to several places – Canada, he thought. But he was in a place with all these books out and he saw this one on Australia, so he thought, I'll go to Australia.

I always said he was for me. He was the only boy I felt I could go out with. He was ten years older than me. There was a couple of others hangin' after me, but I wouldn't go out with 'em – just had the feelin' I didn't want to be bothered with them. But when Len came along I felt I could go with him, quite leisurely you know, quite happy. Eighteen months, courting. We'd just go walking. There *was* the pitcha house up in Meekatharra, but it was mainly things to do with the church where we went.

Meekatharra was where we was married. A two-tier dress, not a long white dress, but a pretty one, and a pitcha hat – the organist made my hat and I think she made my frock too. (Those are nearly all wedding presents I had, over there.) I remember comin' out of the church and I had me head down, because they threw rice in those days. And someone lifts up my head and *kissed* me – who it was, I don't know until this day! Then we had a trap and went for a drive and I had the spread at home. The baker living opposite made my cake, a double-decker thing.

At night, having come home from the mine, my husband used to have a bath. We had no bathroom, so we'd have to put the bath out and the water come out of the tank so hot that you'd have to let it cool. They used to come round with water; you'd order it and put it in big tanks. Not much rain there. (Not like here!) We had water bags hangin' up to keep the water cool to drink.

The mine was a good way out from town. My husband used to ride his bicycle out there. Then he'd come back at night and I'd cook his dinner. Oh, we were quite happy. My youngest sister stayed with me for a long time. She was terribly fond of my husband – he was fond of her too – she was a good kid. She wanted to come over 'ere with us, she cried and cried when we went. My 'usband would have brought her I think. We asked my father, but he said 'No.' He said one was bad enough to go away, he said. He didn't worry about me, he said, because he knew I had a good husband and would be looked after, but he couldn't spare no more of them, he said. She married eventually. She had three children and one of her daughters in Kalgoorlie writes to me every Christmas – she writes lovely letters – she's the only one I hear from out there now.

My husband's aunt wanted him to come Home; she was livin' on her own and she was beggin' for him to come Home. She had a small holding down at Gower [South Wales]. So his mother and father [in Swansea] sent for him. His father was getting on and he had all these gardens at the back [of the house] so they wanted him to carry on – there was only him and his brother.

We were down at Gower about six years, I think (my daughter was born down there, the other two were born in Swansea). Then we came into this house; his father wanted to give up here. His father and us are the only ones been in this house.

We went from Meekatharra and spent a week in Perth in the

131

big coffee palace, for a honeymoon (we didn't have one at the time we were married). Then we went to Albany where we left for over here. War was declared while we were on ship. We only had one light because the Germans were waiting for us – the ship in front of us was sank. So we went out of our route and some couldn't get off where they wanted to. It *was* scaring and they were all very anxious over here. No, we didn't know anything about the war, or I don't suppose we'd have come.

We grew flowers here – had greenhouses up the back – and used to make wreaths and he attended the market Friday and Saturdays. I attended the market in the First World War, when he was in the army. I didn't like him going off to the war but you just had to put up with it.

He was in the army two years, out in France. He was discharged because he had five wounds, one in his shoulder, in his knee (his knee was never straight after) and his finger was blown off. No, he didn't ever tell me how it happened. My brother was killed in the war, at that Gallipoli place.

My father died up in Meekatharra. He was seventy-six and he had nobody with him when he died. All the girls were miles away – I was over here of course. They sent for one of the girls, but it was too late – you see they die one day and they bury the next because it's so hot, they can't keep 'em. So none of them went to him, couldn't get to him. I often think about that – I looked after him *so long* and then there was *nobody* with him when he died. That's the way it is out there, you see.

I never seen any of my sisters again, they're all gone now. I was cut off from them altogether. It was my own fault, my 'usband would have gone back to Australia. When we were in Gower, he asked me would I like to go back to Australia. When he was here in bed ill, before he died, he said he was worried to think he brought me all this way over here, away from all my people. And I said he needn't worry, I'd been very happy here and I hadn't regretted it. He said, 'We'll meet again some day I hope,' he said when he was dying. But I don't know, I think I'm a long time coming! I'm eighty-nine now you see! I didn't think I'd live this long.

But he was a good husband and I was one that you could put me down in a place and I'm settled. I didn't want to be flying about, not like they are now, some of them. I never regretted it – I enjoyed my life, quiet as it was. We just enjoyed home life, I suppose.

I haven't been out for eight years. I've got congestion on the lungs. I'm all right though I'm completely deaf in one ear. And if my eyes would keep all right – but when they go . . . Otherwise, I'm not so bad, except I can't see properly.

I had a man come here the other day to fix the telephone. He just finished off and he said, 'Excuse me, what part of Australia did you come from? I can tell by your talk!' I said 'After all these years!' And I never thought I had any accent!

I quite enjoyed all my life. I've always enjoyed it over here. I got on very well with his people, his mother and father was alive. I had 'em here and I looked after 'em when they was ill – and his aunt. And I had a good husband and I had a good father, he looked after us all.

The Old Head Nurse

And speaking of nurses, now's my chance
To put in a word for the sisterhood.
Their life has little or no romance,
The work is grand and their hearts are good.

But I want you to know that preachers and pugs,
Doctors and editors (publishers too)
Likewise spielers and also mugs
And nurses *and poets have hearts like you.*

— Henry Lawson

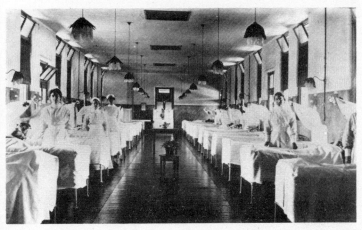

Perth Public Hospital, ward interior, 1919

Aboriginals dressed in kangaroo skins and carrying
game, 1880s

According to records, in 1890, four nurses and two servants were hired at the Colonial Hospital in Perth by the day. Night staff, however, were 'engaged as required'. The nurses earned £30 per annum, a little less than the £45 per annum achieved by the nurses at the lunatic asylum. The official duties of a nurse at the asylum included supervising the household work of patients such as drawing water, amusing the patients by games of cricket or draughts and restraining the unruly by means of camisole straitjackets or the use of handmuffs.

Although there are many individual tales of the dedication of nurses, going to hospital in the colonies was probably an experience to be avoided if possible in the nineteenth century. Hospital nurses were unskilled and untrained. Records indicate that many nurses were women who rarely washed and who tippled on the side. Until Florence Nightingale's ideas reached the colonies, nursing was a trade with no skill and little grace. Miss Nightingale fought for the idea of nursing as a vocation which required special training and gradually Nightingale training schools were introduced into the major hospitals in the colonies and nurses changed from rough labourers into dedicated and knowledgeable ladies.

By the time the farmer's daughter went to hospital as a trainee nurse, nursing was viewed as a vocation. A Nightingale trainee had come to the Perth Hospital in 1888 and entry was restricted to respectable young women who could provide a reference from a clergyman. Training was provided in return for poor wages, a ten-to-twelve-hour working day and rigid off-duty discipline. Since the primary objection to Florence Nightingale introducing her form of nursing was that it was an immoral occupation, it is scarcely surprising that the convent was used as the model for accommodation for nurses in training.

The farmer's daughter spent her working life as a nurse and retired eventually as matron of a private nursing home. After retirement she met a man she had known in her youth in her home town of Katanning. In her seventies, she married and now the husband finds himself caring for the nurse, as she has recently been inflicted with a serious, debilitating illness and is nearly blind.

After I was born at Albany, in 1896, my father and mother took me to Clear Hills near Katanning, the farm father bought from his father-in-law, who had built it. There was a large house built from granite on the property with three bedrooms, a sitting-room, dining-room, a large kitchen and store-room, in which was stored half a ton of sugar, three or four chests of tea, six bags of rice and thousands of tins of Nestlé milk (which came from Switzerland in those days). Albany was our nearest base and there were only horse-drawn vehicles, so a big stock was kept in the store. English beef was available in those days in casks – salted. We had about six of those and that would last a long time. In the kitchen, there was a baker's oven. We grew our own vegetables, but fruit was very seldom seen – the first fruit I ever tasted were apricots and oranges when I was five or six. At Clear Hills my father farmed wheat, oats and barley. He also ran pigs, fowls, ducks and geese.

There was a little cemetery which was treated very sacredly by us. My mother saw it was fenced and paled and always painted white. They were child relatives who were buried there. In the bush there were native graves; I remember seeing them as a child. When a relative died, they'd bury them. I believe they sat them up and left their mug and a tin plate on the grave.

The natives were interesting people, although we were a bit afraid of them as children. They walked from farm to farm, about fifteen or twenty together. Coobie was the oldest native, a pleasant-faced old lady who never used a comb and who had a little bag – a coot – in which she carried her treasures. She also carried a baby on her back and usually asked for sugar, flour and 'baccy'. My mother was very generous to them; they liked one another and we shared what we had with them. The farmers around were all good to the natives. You'd see them coming up the hill, one would come to the door, 'Missus, have you any sugar/tea/flour?' My mother never said no. The farmers liked the natives. I don't know why they liked them, they took them for what they were. My father always said the natives, especially the women, were very kind people towards us. The men may have been a bit warlike – to know their country was invaded, it was a natural thing, but they weren't vicious.

The native didn't work. He might have done a bit of shepherd work – there were no fences in those days. They protected the sheep from mainly wild dogs, and saw they didn't stray.

Their wives were chosen for them by the elders – no marriage with the whites, not even liaisons. They just seemed to be separate people and one respected the other. I remember the natives when they wore kangaroo skins, one arm free for movement and they always carried a digging stick (they didn't have knives). They could camp in the bush anywhere; nobody told them where to go. Such vast lands, uncultivated and unfenced, they had their camping grounds, but they wandered.

Now about entertainment. The men went tammer hunting (the tammer is a small animal, like the kangaroo) and duck shooting. The women used to go and take a picnic and sat around talking. The children just played. I can't remember being bored. Duck shooting provided a luxurious meal now and again. And the tammer – have you ever tasted kangaroo? I couldn't eat it now, but then it was eaten like steak. I've also eaten possum meat, the most delicious thing. My mother used to bake it. We'd have it to make a change.

On this farm the chaff-cutters came. The chaff-cutter was a great big cumbersome engine with a funnel and it burnt wood and the steam engine was used to cut chaff. Don't ask me to explain how it worked. Mr Sheer and his men used to travel round the country with this great chaff-cutter.

Eventually my father sold Clear Hills and built a property twelve miles west of Katanning, which he named Cheviot Hills. A beautiful river running through the property left lovely pools in the summer. The property also grew wheat and there was a clay brick house and a stable for twelve horses. My mother went down to the river to do the laundry. Kerosene tins boiled the clothes and the old fashioned, galvanized tubs were used to bleach the clothes. They were left to dry by the river. For us children, washing day was like a picnic. We'd have a picnic lunch down there. There were gilgies [similar to small lobsters] in the river, quite nice eating. Turtles were plentiful and water-hens and falcons lived in the rushes with their chicks. There were many snakes, but they never gave us any trouble. We seemed to live in peace together. I can't remember being careful; we used to run through the bush – mostly without shoes – but none of us were bitten by any creature. Great carpet snakes – we left things alone – we never touched them and they didn't trouble us. I never felt afraid of snakes or any creatures in the bush.

My father left a well-established farm to live one mile from Katanning at a farm named after our oldest horse. This property was established as a model farm by a Dutchman. It was a small, full-scale farm, milking sheds, lovely grazing property and a chaff-cutter and a blacksmith shop with great bellows – they were at least twelve feet long.

There were twelve hundred vines, with about twenty kinds of grapes, acres of mixed fruits and an acre of different sorts of apples. You wouldn't see these now. They only grow about four different kinds in Western Australia on account of fruit fly.

The fruit was just for the family. My mother used to dry the fruit for raisins. We also had currant pies. My father never sold a pound of anything; he gave it to hospitals and the natives used to always be coming; they got well fed so none was wasted.

We had a lovely flower garden laid out beautifully in all shapes – diamonds and things. We had a lot of bulbs, daffodils mostly and annuals and white lillies all the way round the fence. Marigold, stocks and wallflowers – they had a great respect for England.

We went to school in Katanning, attended church and Sunday school. Our social life was nice – a tennis court on the property and I remember learning to sing and dance. We used to have musical evenings or afternoons at different homes either with our own age group or with older people.

Then World War I came. Such a lot of men went from Katanning. They went voluntarily. When war was declared, they realized how dangerous it was for their country – they wouldn't have any farms. They usually left someone behind to run the farm – if there were four brothers, three would go to the war and one would stay on the farm. It meant women did do more on the farm if the men went, but it seemed to me that these young men who went to the war had fathers who still carried on the farm.

By that time, it was 1916 and I was helping my mother. My father didn't want us to work at all and to stay home. It was the way he was brought up. But my mother thought it was sensible to do something. My father's ambition was to get us to England, to finishing school, but he could never afford it.

Nursing was my ambition. I wanted to look after people. Nursing was considered a good thing. You were doing something for someone not able to help themselves. I knew my father was proud of me. Nurses were expected to bring a letter of introduction from three prominent people, including a minister. I don't know how many were refused; maybe some were. I know the girls I went in with were, looking back on them, very respectable people. I think they came from those kind of families: now it's a different story!

At Perth Hospital, we went straight into the wards. There

were two juniors in a ward, two seniors, the staff nurse and the sister. As a junior, you were not allowed to speak to a sister until she spoke to you. If I were sent across to the dispensary and saw a sister I knew, I never spoke. But it was accepted. She was the sister, you respected her. Off-duty we had to be in by 10 o'clock or report at matron's office if we were later: on one day, we were allowed in at eleven. No nonsense allowed on the ward, no talking allowed. There was plenty to do. In any case you stayed there until you finished your work! For example, the women patients had to have their hair done in a certain way – it was parted in the centre in two plaits, one on each side, and that was the junior's job. If their hair wasn't tidy – the sister would just look down the row and if she saw a patient's head untidy, she made the nurse do it properly.

We used to have lectures. Matron's lectures were mostly on hygiene and hospital behaviour. Then we would have lectures from a doctor who was a surgeon and from a medical man. We did our work, starting at 7 o'clock. At two in the afternoon we had a few hours off and then we'd go back at six. By 10 o'clock you came off.

Each junior was expected to wash bandages and clean all the lockers every morning, clean the pan room, carry trays. You sponged the patients and looked after them generally. You'd have at least ten or twelve typhoid patients. They were only given fluids every two hours – mostly milk foods and dairy products. They had what we called a bath. They were sponged every four hours, a mackintosh was put on the bed and the patient rubbed gently. If their temperature was rising, the doctor used to order two-hourly sponges. And they were nursed in the general wards. We wore gowns and masks, but I can't remember anyone being infected in the ward, or any general patients developing typhoid.

Nurses came in prepared to accept what was asked and to do it with good grace. But they seemed to be happy: I don't remember one unhappy nurse.

The Tail Of a Kangaroo

Now Julia's just the sort of girl to ride a bucking colt,
Or round a mob of cattle up, if they're inclined to bolt
Ride on her brother's saddle all astride or, on a push,
Do any kind of mortal work that's wanted in the bush

— Anon.

Country picnic, Tammin, 1910

By 1890, 148 imperial convicts remained in Western Australia from the earlier period of transportation which ceased in 1868. Four out of ten men were employed on public works and about a quarter had been given a 'ticket-of-leave' to work for private employers. Another quarter had achieved a conditional release, while the rest were classified as invalids or lunatics.

The following account indicates that some convicts had achieved acceptance in the economic life of the community. In a colony desperately short of labour, it was relatively easy for a convict to earn a living. But the grazier's daughter implies that ex-convicts served a social as well as an economic purpose. In a raw, new community where few of the traditional trappings of class were on display, the presence of the ex-convicts provided a clear dividing line between the respectable people and the deviant in the community. For example, the grazier went to read the Bible to an old convict. This action not only defined the old convict as a needy soul, but it also confirmed the grazier's view of himself as the essence of respectability. But the acceptance the ex-convicts did achieve would have been impossible in the more rigid English county life. One wonders if breaking the legal and social rules was tolerated more readily in the Western Australian country than in the English county.

The grazier's daughter was divorced in 1910, when divorce was very uncommon (particularly divorces instigated by women petitioners). Social and financial decline hit the grazier's daughter following the dissolution of her marriage and she moved to the suburbs. In old age, she went to live in a nursing home with the clerk's daughter and the miner's daughter. She seemed a frail woman, but she maintained a straight back, an impeccable southern English accent and a tentative smile. She died shortly after recording her story.

1882 was when I was born. I was the last one in the family and I was born in the bush. The earliest I remember was about five I s'pose. I was a little demon riding things at that age, horses that were quiet enough. I was put on horse-back under the harness, first astride, then I learned to ride side-saddle. You wouldn't ride astride in those days – not done! I was mad about horses as soon as I could get on them. Later, if we had a young horse who was a demon, they'd come and say, 'Would you come hold so and so's head? He won't stand still.' And I'd hold the horse's head and stroke him and he'd be quiet with me. I often had to go with my brother for instance – he was eight years older than me – he'd come and say, 'I want some horses.' Not a lot of land was fenced in, so horses were often running loose and you couldn't walk up and catch one – they're cunning. So they'd be feeding and I'd walk up to them and stroke their forequarters and then my brother could come up quietly behind and catch them. Then he'd put me on the horse, bareback – that *was* astride – he'd jump on and he'd ride the horse home. And that's how I learned to ride.

My mother was born a Scotswoman, from Arbroath. The family went to live in England at Kidderminster which was a carpet town. I don't know what went wrong with their business, but it went crash. The eldest son came out to Australia and got into the bank, the National Bank and after being here a year or two, he sent for the rest of the family. The second son went to America to other carpet people there. And the remaining children came out here to Australia – five girls and four boys! The one who was here in the National Bank got positions for the father and one of the sons in South Australia. My mother was twelve when she arrived at Kangaroo Island in South Australia.

Father was Surrey, he lived at Farnham; they were well-to-do. He was sent out to Australia by his father who was a doctor. Father developed a cough and his parents were afraid he was getting T.B. His father had a friend out here in South Australia, on the border of South Australia and Victoria and he had a cattle station. So he sent father off as a jackeroo –and father was there for sixteen years. He arrived when he was twenty-two, just when the goldfields were raging. He learned how to handle cattle. Somehow he met during those times with the Joneses,. and mother married him when she was eighteen. Father was twenty years older than she. Father bought a station called 'Gee Geela' and they were living there – I don't know for how long – and they had a drought in South Australia and stock were dying. Meanwhile, my eldest uncle had come to West Australia as the manager of the National Bank here. And he had on the books a property for sale as someone was getting out – he wrote to father and told him to buy this property. So father came here, knowing nothing at all about box poison and the stock were in foot and mouth. So he said, 'I wouldn't buy a place like that: poison . . .' Someone else bought it (who knew how to handle the poison) and father bought another property.

So they lived there for a couple of years and a daughter was born but died in infancy. Then my brother was born there. He didn't die – in fact he lived until he was twenty-two – he didn't die until typhoid broke out on the Kalgoorlie goldfields. He had taken his team up to 'cart' things (you could get fantastic prices for foreign goods), and he got typhoid and died. He telegraphed down to say he was sick and mother got on the train and brought him home. But the doctor said he couldn't live.

I was fifteen when my brother died. Until I was about twelve years old, I had governesses. But I was used to the farm and used to riding and I didn't see why I should be inside learning things in books, and I'm afraid I gave my governesses a rare old time. I just lived a wild life – I was a wild little creature. No girlfriends at all. When I got to twelve, my parents said, 'This has got to stop – she's got to go to school.'

And I boarded out at a farmer's place, about a mile from the school, the government school. I was very unhappy – I used to cry myself to sleep every night, so my parents left the farm. Father and mother rented a house not far from school and I could walk. It was heavenly, of course, to get back to mother.

The first day of school . . . I didn't know any of the rules . . . I did not say 'good-bye' or 'good afternoon' and I was called back and caned [laughs]. I'd never been caned in my life. I was taught to read to a certain extent at school – the chief thing was books of poetry, I had to learn poetry . . . quite good books, in comparison with the twaddle I hear about today. English history . . . no Australian . . . there wasn't any. I was taught to sew and as the years went on, I was given jobs training the younger ones – hemming, top sewing. I *think* I enjoyed school . . . I was rather a loner. We were always dressed in a pinafore, a white pinafore with lace trimming around here.

When I left school – I was fifteen – I was given the job of teaching the little ones – teaching their ABC and all that. They called them monitors. I got paid £16 a year – I thought I earned it! They had one class from babyhood – four or five – up to twelve or fourteen – there was one boy who was nearly a man in size.

I did the job about a year I think. Then I had a music teacher at home, an English R.A.M. woman – she came out to meet the man she had married – so the story goes. But he died journeying to England on a ship. She had one child. In those days things were conservative, and she never wore a wedding ring for one thing, so people thought the child was illegitimate. Those sort of things happened . . . she belonged to a very good family in England and I think she got away!

Things were very cliquey in those days. We had dances in Pingelly and they were public, so I don't remember restrictions on who could come, but you only talked to friends or friends of friends. For example, you wouldn't think of going to have a meal at a table with someone else who had been a servant of the family. There was one case where the

148

mother had married beneath her – married a servant or
something – and the children of that family ate in the kitchen
if they went to the house. Oh yes, they were very cliquey in
those days . . . They might have mixed and talked, but they
didn't come into your drawing room; one didn't ask them to
the dinner table. A lot of very good families came out here
from good English homes and they kept it up . . . strictly
gentlemen and yet they were workmen too. There were class
distinctions – the man who was our teamster had his meals in
the kitchen of course; it's changed now, things are different
now. People who were beneath one are quite alright now!
There was one old couple – I think he came out as a convict
in the convict era – he and his wife were old and blind and
my father used to go to read the Bible to them on a Sunday,
sometimes. But those people *now* would have lots of things
and a lovely home – it's quite different.

I met convicts very often. There was one built our house.
He was a carpenter-sort-of-man, and he used to do jobs for
everybody. Convicts were first of all ticket-of-leave and if they
behaved themselves, they got a free pass. He had a lot of
children who went to the same school as I went to. He was a
very aristocratic-looking man – nice, tall, well set up man.
What he was before, in England, I don't know. Another old
man, who was ticket-of-leave, used to go around and buy
sheepskins from people on the farms. There was a blacksmith
with a shop. It wasn't a secret, they couldn't help people
knowing. Sometimes in those days the police used to stop you
in your buggy and say, 'Bond or free?' They had to see
whether you were bond, so they could check if you were
behaving yourself. If you were free, that was all right.

A lot of people passing through were teamsters, but they
were *not* the same as visitors! We had not many visitors, as we
were twenty-five miles from the nearest town, Pingelly. Horses
did about six miles an hour then. The teamsters used to come
up past us and stop there for the night, camping near our
water for their horses. We'd supply them with bread and
bacon, and they'd buy some butter as part of their tucker for

the trip. They were going further on to where the sandalwood was cut. It was sent to China in those days for incense. A wagon with four horses carted it to Fremantle to the wharf and sold it to merchants and they shipped it away to China. Beautiful smell!

As a child I had no children to play with – only black children. They used to dig up roots and look for grubs and they were quiet and nice. The blacks used to come around and camp a little way from the house. They used to do jobs – mother had one of them as a nursemaid when I was a tiny child. If one of the camps had a sick man, mother used to make some soup and take it to him until he died. Our people got on well with the natives – there was no trouble at all. They'd do the work – clear trees out, that sort of thing. They'd stay for a week or a fortnight and be gone in the morning.

They had no culture at all. They had a language of their own, you could learn it after a fashion . . . They had no culture but certain things were thought to be known to them, about the stars and things like that. But they couldn't count past three . . . They were regarded very much as inferior. Father was walking along the road one day and he found a man – a black man – tied to a tree. So he unloosed him and let him go. And he said that a certain man – a white man – had tied him to the tree and left him to die. Father reported it to the police. So the white man was had up, but they didn't do much in those days to punish, they'd have punished him in some small way. If it was a white man tied up, it'd have been another matter. The black man didn't matter.

After that, well, a man came out from England and I met him on the farm. He had failed to pass his last exam as a doctor and he came out here and bought a farm. I became engaged to him. He got sick and he died. He had a toothache and being a student doctor he had some laudanum – and he must have taken an overdose. He and another man went out to get in some cattle that were running loose and they were to camp at a certain place and he didn't turn up that night. They found him next morning, unconscious and he died. I was terribly upset . . . I was eighteen . . . it was a long while before I married.

After my fiancé died, we went to England to see his people – Rochester in Kent; they're all dead now. Fares to England were cheap then – you only had to pay about £30 for a return fare. We got to England just a day or two before the coronation in 1902 and it was cancelled. So we went on the continent and saw Switzerland by horse – no motor cars then (the motor car had just come into America when we were there – nasty smelly things, frightened the horses!). We went to Switzerland, over the mountains there to Lucerne. The bridge there out on the lake – oh, I thought it all very wonderful, although I did want to see it snow. But when we arrived in the middle of January, it had stopped and by the time we got to America in March, it had stopped. Lucerne – Mount Blanc – all so interesting.

It was exciting to get to London and see all these old, old buildings everywhere you looked. I was *terribly* Australian. I wouldn't have anything said about Australia that wan't the ideal place. I never met many English girls. Mother had a friend there who had daughters – they used to go to dancing and parties and I wouldn't. I went to one dance. I'm sure they thought I was different, but they were too well brought up to say so!

We were a patriotic family, as to Australia. We went on to America to my other uncle and I used to fight with my cousins there like anything for Australia – just as good as America! Australia first and England came second.

Then we came back to Australia, to our farm. We'd let it while we were away. My job was helping, helping my mother and my father. When my mother didn't need help in the house, I'd go out and ride around the sheep, or the cattle, or whatever needed looking after. I carted the hay and helped pitch sheaths of hay. I did a man's job, I was never very fat – eight stone that's all. You were short of so many men, so I used to go in there and do all sorts of things.

Then I met my future husband at a friend's house and I

didn't know then that he was an alcoholic. He was very charming. I knew him two years before I married and I never knew. I was trapped in a way – I always saw him sober, until I got married. When my eldest child was five years old, he had a drinking bout and he frightened the life out of me. I was going to have another baby and I was pretty sick, I had to get a doctor in. And the menfolk of the township got hold of him and told him – they thought I was not going to live – they got at him and told him that if I died, they'd have him up for manslaughter. And he cleared out. I never saw him again. He stayed away a year. Then I saw somebody who saw him and she heard that he was coming to take the children away from me and that frightened me. I got a good lawyer in Perth who listened to my case and said, 'Get a divorce,' and I did. Of course, fathers were legal guardians in those days and they could do as they wished. It must have been another four or five years before I got the divorce, about 1910.

In those days with a divorce you were outski! Some friends stuck to me, some didn't. You'd done something you shouldn't do. I still went to church, my children went and they were confirmed. They were sympathetic. But you were often left alone and left out of everything, you weren't nice to know. I suppose it upset me at the time.

I found out afterwards that he was really an alcoholic before he left Scotland and he had a quarrel with family and he cleared out of Scotland and worked all over the world. His father was a ship's chandler and his mother must have quarrelled with him and slapped his face. He was a very charming man, could be very charming. But he was really aggressive. He used to lie in a room and drink and I'd have to tell the men employed on the farm what to do – he just left it. I had all the responsibility with mother and father. It was very much easier after he went away because we got a manager in to work the farm.

He was full of fun and full of games when he wasn't drinking, but you never knew when he was going to. He had a friend who was an alcoholic too, and he'd come in to the place with a bottle of whisky and say, 'Come on there, have a drink,' and they'd start off. Once I went into the room and to hide the bottle, he poured it over the flowers.

Oh, we had fights about it – he wasn't going to do it anymore, he wasn't going to do it again. After four days he reeked again; he'd come home again from town, drunk and that was that! When he'd say 'I'll kill everyone,' I was frightened. Other women put up with that all their lives – I wonder why. I'd never had much to do with people who were like that; I couldn't put up with it, I couldn't stand it.

The children lacked the help a father would give, there was no doubt about that. My parents did help support me and I had no money, but I could sew. I had the advantage of having good parents, and father and mother owned the property. I stayed with them till they died and after they died, they left it to me and I sold it, after that. Really, how it came to be 'sold' was that we were mortgaged, of course; I had to get used to buying for the farm, sheep and things. We mortgaged the property to get the money, and the droughts came and everything went dead. The wool went down to one shilling a pound and the wheat . . ! We couldn't pay the interest, so they took the property. About 1915, I think. Tough times, they were.

My life was pretty mixed. I was happy in a way, but I liked helping myself, I don't like being closed in. The marriage was the break. I thought marriage was romantic when I got married. Now I think it's very doubtful. When I hear of people getting married I think, 'I hope they're happy.' I'm glad I never tried it again. In some cases it works – I knew a family in Pingelly and they were as happy as happy all their lives – yet others go to pieces so quickly. They have unhappy lives and they don't want to talk about it – they're disillusioned, I think. In those days you thought things were what they were – and they weren't; you thought people were a certain sort and they were not that really. For example you thought people were nicer than they were, that they wouldn't do things they shouldn't do. You considered you were the first person in their life and you weren't.

My daughter had an unhappy life; her husband was no good and she divorced him after putting up with him for ten years. Then she and I shared a house in Perth for many years until she died of terrible cancer of the back. She was only in hospital for five weeks before she died; they can give them these pills now to keep the pain away. That was seven years ago. That's when I came in here, into this home. The latter part of my life has been quite happy.

A one-teacher country school

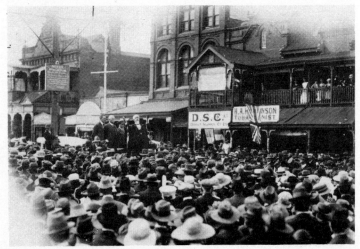

Recruiting for volunteers for World War I, 1917

Nursery Rhyme

One year, two year, three year, four,
Comes a khaki gentleman knocking at the door;
Any little boys at home? Send them out to me,
To train them and brain them in battles yet to be.
Five year, six year, seven year, eight,
Hurry up, you little chaps, the captain's at the gate.

When a little boy is born, feed him, train him, so;
Put him in a cattle pen and wait for him to grow;
When he's nice and plump and dear, sensible and sweet,
Throw him in the trenches for the grey rats to eat;
Toss him in the cannon's mouth, cannons fancy best
Tender little boy flesh, that's easy to digest.

One year, two year, three year, four,
Listen to the generals singing out for more!
Soon he'll be a soldier-boy, won't he be a toff,
Pretty little soldier, with his head blown off!

Mother rears her family on two pounds a week,
Teaches them to wash themselves, teaches them to speak,
Rears them with a heart's love – rears them to be men,
Grinds her fingers to the bone – then, what then?

One year, two year, three year, four,
Comes a khaki gentleman knocking at the door;
Little boys are wanted now very much indeed,
Hear the bugles blowing when the cannons want a feed!
Fowl-food, horse-food, man-food are dear,
Cannon fodder's always cheap, conscript or volunteer.

– Furnley Maurice

She was born in 1887, and the story of her early life is valuable because of her social observation and dissection of the social attitudes of the upper middle classes of Victorian colonial society and the subsequent Edwardian period to the close of the First World War. But the First World War was 'the second war' to the accountant's daughter because she remembers the Boer War as the 'first war'.

She became a teacher. For the well-bred young woman in a small colonial society, there were few occupational outlets. Many women, including the daughters of the magistrate and the archbishop, stayed at home. For the rest, teaching was about the only admissable respectable, paid occupation. But teacher training for women brought attendant risks in elevating female knowledge and status above accepted levels. As Donald Rankin, educational historian writing after the First World War, said:

It is easy to understand that many men of the world would be nervous about encouraging marriage with an educated lady teacher. They forget that the essence of culture is to know when to use knowledge and when not to. Experience shows that the teachers trained by the various departments make excellent wives . . . On one occasion, when travelling by steamer to Perth, I was introduced to a young lady, apparently just entering her third decade of life and who, I was told, was a young teacher in the employ of the Education Department of Western Australia. This young lady was one of the most cultured I have ever spoken to. It would be difficult to do justice to her in a few words, but I mentally praised the educational system that produced such a pleasing result. Her exact and varied knowledge, her balanced intellect, her careful enunciation and her easy and graceful manners made me realise my own limitations. Two years later we were again passengers on the same boat but my cultured lady was now playing another role. My first acquaintance was with a scholar; the second time, the scholar was there, but it threw out into better relief the new phase of 'mother'.

The question of appropriate occupations for women at the turn of the century in a small colonial society cannot be separated from the relevance of such training to the central theme of motherhood.

The marriage of the accountant's daughter was short-lived and not very happy. Widowed, she taught for most of her working life. She remembers a time when the policy of 'payment by results' for teachers made their rewards dependent on the attendance and examination performance of their pupils. In scattered rural communities, irregular attendance of pupils was always a hazard and the emphasis on exam results made teachers overly dependent on promoting mechanical habits and learning by rote.

As this record indicates, the accountant's daughter, at the age of ninety-three has a remarkably active brain and vivid recall. She is, however, confined permanently to hospital, as she is unable to manage alone. She is bedridden because she is crippled by arthritis, almost completely deaf and nearly blind. The casual visitor might be forgiven for passing quickly by her bed. Although she can talk articulately, her visitors need to write their messages in large black print on a pad. She spends each day under the direction of nurses who control her rising, dressing and eating. She is returned to bed for the night at 3 o'clock each day and required permission from the matron to have me visit her. Her other companions in the ward are senile, incontinent and noisy, so she is unable to communicate with others. Given her past record as woman and citizen and her present mental vitality and spirit, her end is a deep sorrow to her.

I was born in a street called Limbo Street in Perth. We had a two-storeyed house right opposite the gaol. The night before I was born, my mother said she was in an upstairs room with the nurse. 'What's all that hammering going on?' she said. And the nurse said, 'They're putting up the gallows, they're going to hang a man in the morning.' So I arrived here in this sphere at 3 o'clock in the morning and a man went out of this sphere at 8 o'clock in the morning, but he went out by the gallows. I came in and he went out almost simultaneously. That was December 1887.

We were a lovely family – there were 7 of us, I was the middle one. My father used to work in the Supreme Court; he was an accountant in bankruptcy. He was there about forty years until he retired. My father was the highest paid accountant in Perth – £5 a week and he had seven children. My mother came from a wealthy family – the Huddart-Parker shipping company. They were all wealthy – there was money galore there. They had a shipping company in England and they started another in Australia. They said that if my mother married my father, they'd cut her off entirely as he'd never be anything but a struggling accountant. Well, they cut her off and she got no help at all from her family. Much later, Uncle Gardiner Huddart came to Perth for Huddart-Parker, on his way to Egypt for the winter. He ordered champagne and made it up with my mother! My mother was a very pretty woman. My father used to say there wasn't a girl in Ballarat to match her. She was very beautiful and had a long swan like neck. We used to call her Queen Alexandra, because of the neck. My father came from Victoria; his father had been the headmaster at Geelong Grammar. My father was at school until he was eighteen and he was mad on education. In many ways, he was very English.

We were in Limbo Street for four years. I believe I was four when my father bought a property in Palmerston Street, which was then one of the aristocratic streets of Perth, where all the doctors and lawyers and bankers lived. We lived opposite the Postmaster General, Mr Brooking. Mr Brooking used to go to work on a penny farthing – I used to look through the bars of the gate every morning to see him go past – a great big wheel in the front and a little tiny wheel at the back.

We lived next door to Palmerston Park, a beautiful house, standing in an acre of grounds. It had iron railings, brick work

up to there, then iron railings with spikes. The owner brought
all the fittings in the house from England; the drawing room
was lined with polished oak panels. That was quite different to
our own house which was just an ordinary brick villa, with
about five rooms, but very nice for the time. So many houses
in those days were made of wood – my father wouldn't have a
wooden house.

We lived very well. We used to visit Government House –
my father and mother used to go to dinner there very often.
My mother was young – just one baby at the time when they
were at a dinner party at Government House one night – and
they were talking about the convicts. Of course, West Australia
was its own colony then – we didn't federate until 1901 – and
it was the home of convicts in those days. They'd sent some
out from England to Western Australia. My mother said, 'You
never know nowadays if you're rubbing shoulders with a
ticket-of-leave man.' My father nudged her to keep quiet,
because she was actually sitting next to a ticket-of-leave man.
That means a man who was never allowed to leave the colony.
They were convicts who were allowed to have their freedom
but never to leave the colony.

The story was that he had been sent out on some trifling
thing – he'd made some remark about Queen Victoria and
they called it treason. He was a Member of Parliament, but he
was sent out on a boat with all the criminals; then he was
freed but he was never allowed to go back to England. We
lived near another M.P. who was put into jail for three months
because he spoke treason against the queen. He got three
months' gaol and while he was there, they shaved his head. So
he swore he'd never have scissors put on his hair again. And
when he came out he let it grow; it was down to his shoulders
when we children used to know him – lovely brown hair with
a curl to it. They were very touchy about royalty in those days.
Nowadays they say what they like!

There wasn't any special interest taken in Aboriginal ways
when I was young. The black was black and the white was
white and never the twain shall meet. My mother had a black

washer-woman – she lived with a white man. He was beyond
the pale altogether, the white man who would live with a
lubra. Many a Monday she didn't turn up. The police would
run her in over the weekend and she'd get seven days for
drunk and disorderly. But she was a marvellous washer-
woman. 'You didn't come last Monday,' my mother would
say. She'd say, 'I not well, Missus.' Actually she used to be in
gaol. Don't forget there were no laundries like now. We all
had an outside wash-house with troughs in it and a copper.
You had a fire under the copper – the clothes were always
boiled. It was a big job in those days.

When I was a child, the blacks had camps around Perth and
they were practically beggars; they had no payments from the
government to keep them. If my father was late coming home
– he sometimes used to be back at work and sometimes out
playing cards – my mother wouldn't go to bed until he came
home. One very cold, wet night she was sitting by the fire in
the dining-room and there was a hammering on the front
door. 'Missus, missus, let me in. I'm cold, I've got no clothes.'
She wasn't going to open the door to a black man with no
clothes on. She called out, 'Go to the back and get some wood
for a fire.'

I don't think that blacks and whites had anything to do with
one another. Blacks kept to themselves; they had their camps
and lots of dogs – kangaroo dogs, tall skinny things. There was
a creek at the foot of our hill, where there was a blacks' camp.
They used to come begging. Some men used to go out
working – the men used to chop wood while the women did
washing. There were very few half-castes around Perth, it
wasn't the custom for a black man to live with a white woman
or vice versa.

As a matter of fact here, every Friday night now, we're given
over to the blacks at 5 o'clock. Black nurses, black everything.
I woke up one night, felt someone touch me and got the fright
of my life. I saw these two big eyes with whites around and a
mouthful full of shining white teeth in this black face. She
laughed like anything: 'I frightened you,' she said.

I started school very young, I was just five. Teachers were very different in those old days. I was very much in awe of them. They never seemed to be friendly, or joking or anything. Some of them were not very well educated – they were not as highly trained as teachers nowadays. Looking back on them, it seems to me they were glad to take anybody who could read or write properly. When I was eight or nine, I had a teacher who was very cruel. She was also common. I often wondered how she got to be a teacher. My father came to the school once – I'd forgotten my lunch. He went upstairs and had a talk with Miss Girdlestone, the head teacher of Perth Girls. She was a very cultured woman from Girton College, in England. Then he came to the classroom door and spoke to the teacher and said, 'I'd like to speak with my daughter.' So she called out: 'Irene. Ya father wants ya.' So he said to her, 'Madam, my daughter's name is Iren*ee*.' (It's only the Americans who say Irene, without pronouncing the last syllable. Being a Greek word, every syllable should be pronounced. Being English, my father wanted it right.)

There was no training college for teachers then. If a young woman or man passed through the 8th standard with any honours, they made them pupil teachers, which meant they taught half a day practically helping other teachers. They had a sort of technical school; pupil teachers attended for so many hours a week and then sat for an examination and if they passed they became a full term teacher. But they had no other training, only what they trained on us, on the children, you know.

When I was in standard four, the whole class had to do it again. We all had to repeat because of poor teaching. Whenever the teacher came near us we had to dodge, because she'd spit at you as she talked. She left, thank goodness, to get married!

Being rude to the teacher, giving a pert reply or telling a falsehood were all regarded as misdemeanours. They were very strict. One day when I was in the 4th standard, we had long lists of numbers to add up. When you finished you'd

stand up in your place and she'd say, 'Pencils down.' (Slate
pencils, that was.) She'd call out the answer up to millions,
'Three million, one ninety-two thousand.' I was a bit deaf –
I'd thought everything was right, so I stood up with the
others. She went around, marking, and came to me and said
'You're a cheat: you've got a figure wrong. Go out on the
floor.' I burst into tears of course; it was a terrible thing,
because we were such an honest family and my family
considered the truth was the only way to live. She stood me on
a chair and put a big card on me with CHEAT on it and hung
it round my neck. I was standing on this chair in the middle
of the floor crying. The headmistress came in and said,
'What's Irene doing on the chair?' 'She's a cheat,' said the
teacher. 'Oh,' said the headmistress, 'I've never known that
family to lie or cheat. Let her down at once.' That was the
reputation we had. I had no cheek in me or impudence in
those days – we weren't allowed to be rude at home.

At school, we were stuffed with facts, facts of everything.
You learned your history out of books, it was more
mechanical, the education in those days. The teacher wasn't a
friend, she was someone to be afraid of. You only had to turn
your head and she'd say, 'Go up to the office.' I didn't fall
into that category at all – I'd been too well brought up so I
managed to escape punishment. I don't know what would
have happened if I'd been caned; I don't think I would have
ever got over it – the indignity would have lasted me all my
life.

When I was just six, I had an ulcer come in my cheek. Our
family doctor was away for a month. He had in his place a
young Melbourne doctor who was very quick with the knife.
He put everyone to the knife, whereas our doctor would heal
without. He said to my father, 'We must cut that ulcer out.'
My father said, 'You're not going to put a knife on my little
girl's face.' 'Oh yes,' the doctor said, 'it might get roots and go
worse.' I was terrified but he cut all the nerves going to that
ear, that's how I started to go a little bit deaf. My face was
hollow with a lot of flesh cut away. When our doctor came

back he was ropable. He said all that was wanted was a bad
tooth pulled out and the lump would have gone away in a
week. I was dragged to the Royal Perth Hospital every day and
they'd tear the dressings off my face and make it bleed again.
I used to cry the moment I got in and the Scotch nurse would
say, 'I'm not hurrrting yer – stop yer cryin'. There was no
children's hospital in those days.

Children were not the main feature of living in those days –
children were sublimated under all those other things that
came first. The children came last. Such as, if you weren't very
well, you still had to go to Sunday school, with your toothache
and your face swollen up and nearly crying with pain. But you
must never miss Sunday school and school. It doesn't matter
what you suffered, you suffered it and did your job whatever it
was, even if you were only so high. Things have altered a great
deal now, because a child is the pivot of everything nowadays,
much to their ruination, a lot of them. They're far too spoiled;
they have far too much given to them and they are very
insolent to their parents. The training of children is a matter
of how the parents live . . . it comes from the home not
anywhere else.

From the time I was five before I went to school I could
read. My father had a library in his study which was lined with
books. Once I was sitting there, curled up reading, on the
hearthrug, when my father came in with a gentleman friend.
The gentleman looked over my shoulder and said, 'You don't
allow that child to read a book like that?' My father said, 'She
can read anything in this room. If she understands it, it shows
she's old enough to read it. If she doesn't understand it, it
won't hurt her.' That was very sensible of him, wasn't it? He
never had any hard and fast rules about literature. He had a
wonderful library. We had a two-storey barn in the backyard
– the bottom half had my father's horse and the top half was
storage. Everything we didn't want. My grandfather was a
minister and all his books and papers were there. If I was
missing, I was always up there. My mother would call me and
I wouldn't ever hear her, I'd be so engrossed in grandfather's

books. He was rewriting the Bible in a new translation in
longhand – he hadn't finished it when he died. He used to
make long 's' like a 'f' in very black ink on thick, thick paper.

I read all the girls' books, *Red Rose, White Rose* and *Uncle
Tom's Cabin.* It couldn't have been difficult to get books in
Perth because we had plenty. We had the *Caskets of Literature* –
twelve bound volumes – the most fascinating pen and ink
sketches with tissue paper over the sketches. I read everything
I could put my hands on. I remember reading *For the Term of
his Natural Life* in bed, reading it aloud to my younger brother.
We had got up to a most exciting part – where one man ate all
the other men – when my mother came to take the candle
away. So I read the rest with matches – I'd strike a match and
read on until I burnt my fingers. It's a wonder I didn't burn
the house down!

I left school at fifteen in 1902. I didn't go teaching right
away. The Pater said I was to be a teacher: 'You are going to
sit for the teachers' exam and go to the teachers' training
college.' I said, 'I'm not going to be a teacher – he's not going
to make a fool of me.' My two sisters and my older brother
were teachers. So I rebelled. I sat the teachers' exam to go into
the college and I failed. I spoiled all my papers – I was
determined I wouldn't be a teacher. My father was boiling
mad. He said, 'It's the first time a child of mine has ever
failed in an examination.'

I thought it made a fool of the family, everyone being a
teacher – I couldn't stand the stereotype. But I didn't know
what I wanted to do. I thought I'd like to do millinery and
make hats. My father said, 'You cannot do that. You can stay
at home.' I stayed home and helped my mother from when I
was sixteen until I was twenty-six. Ten years! I helped my
mother in the house. It didn't involve very much. Mrs Hassan
came on Tuesday and did the washing and ironing and on
Thursday to clean up the house. We had her for two days a
week and my mother did most of the cooking. My sister and I
were supposed to do a lot of things but mother really did the
most of it. Mother had 'at home' days – her day was a

Thursday, once a month. If my mother visited other houses she always left two cards of her own and one of my father's. It was the correct thing to leave cards in those days. Most people had special 'at home' days where they expected people to come on that day. All the old tabbies used to come! She always used to get me to see to the afternoon tea, because I could make very dainty cucumber sandwiches: I cut the bread very thin – no cut bread in those days. I'd get the afternoon tea ready and put the silver service on a big oak tray and carry it in. I was good on sponges – always a good cook – so I'd slapdash together a passion-fruit sponge.

These elderly women, they were *so* precise. 'Mrs So-and-So, how have you *been* this week?' Oh, a lot of pussy-footing went on you know. These elderly women used to look to me so dowdy – dressed in black with toques on their head, Queen Mary style. Different to my mother, she used to like pretty frocks. I used to go with my mother into town and remember seeing a beautiful cream coloured three-quarter coat, a fluffy coat like lambs-wool, lined with lemon silk. There was no stint on pretty clothes. As my mother's older brothers died, they left her their money.

So I got the coat and used to wear it to dances. I had a lovely social life, I might tell you! We used to have what was called a Long Night every Saturday night. A German woman used to hold the dances in the Town Hall. My brother Rupert and I, a boyfriend of mine and a girl of Rupert's used to go. We'd do the twelve-step right across the lovely polished floor – we'd fly across the hall loving it. We played tennis – I had several friends with tennis courts. We used to have musical evenings where people sang and played the piano. We'd have a singsong and then someone would sing a new song.

My father was a *Victorian* father. Even when I was eighteen, I had to tell him where I was going. For instance, one night, my friend Muriel and I decided to go to town to Her Majesty's Theatre. The dramatic society put on an old-style drama, where a girl is turned out of doors and comes back with a baby in her arms and her father says, 'Begone! You have made your bed, now lie in it!' We used to gulp it all down and wipe our eyes. Of course, our father believed that if you went to the theatre you were chaperoned and you went in evening dress and sat in the front stalls. But we decided we wanted to see this melodrama he didn't believe in. I said to Muriel, 'We'll sit in the gods, it only costs 2s'. We got onto the railway station at West Leederville and my father turned up just before the train came. He was going back to the Supreme Court to do some overflow work at night. 'What are you girls doing here, if I might ask?' We said, 'Oh, we're going to a bazaar at the Wesleyan church, to get money for the Chinese missions.' That was all right, but in fact we went to this terrible play called *Honour Thy Father.* The girl didn't honour her father and she came back with a baby.

She was turned out and we sobbed away, up in the gods. The melodrama didn't come out until half past eleven and we had to run for our lives to get the last train at three minutes to twelve. When we got out, Muriel said my face went as white as a sheet.

'The Pater!' I said. 'There's the Pater on the platform.'

He came up.

'Well,' he said, 'This is a very late hour for little girls to be out.' He was very sarcastic, an early Victorian, you know. 'Where have you been? It's a late hour for a Wesleyan bazaar.'

'Oh,' I said, 'we changed our minds. We didn't go to the bazaar. We thought we'd go to the theatre to see a play.'

He said, 'Oh. What did you see?'

He frightened the life out of me; I couldn't even remember its name. Neither could Muriel. At last I said, *'Honour Thy Father.'*

'Oh,' he said, 'it must be a very fine play with a title like that.'

He had me on toast! He knew very well we went to the theatre purposefully, but he couldn't prove it. He had come down and met every train since 9 o'clock, thinking we'd been at the bazaar. He made a lot of sarcastic remarks about honouring fathers and we were dumb. He said, 'Muriel, I'll

see you home.' To me he said, 'I'll see you in the morning.' I
thought, 'Bejabbers you won't!'

Next morning, my sister said 'The Pater wants to see you.' I
said, 'Tell him I'm not well.' I dodged him for two or three
days and then he forgot about it, so I got off all right!

In those days any girl who had an illegitimate baby was
done for life. No one would speak to her. It was unheard of,
amongst our class anyway. It was the sort of thing that didn't
happen to people like us – you know the sort of arrogant way
the Victorians went on. That sort of thing just *never* happened.
I had a friend who was betrayed by some young man. She
thought she was going to marry him. Anyway he got her into
trouble. Everybody dropped her like a hot coal and she went
down to the jetty and jumped in to the river and drowned
herself because she was going to have an infant and it was a
disgrace. Nowadays they have them right and left and don't
even bother to get married at all. No abortion in those days,
that was murder. It wasn't mentioned in polite society at all;
they were very prim you know.

My father was the Bishop's lay reader and he used to take
services. Once, when we were in the country, in Northam (we
were there for a year when I was fifteen), we drove in a sulky
out to a little tin church; there were only about twenty-five
people there. He went into the vestry to put on his surplice
and as he came through the doorway, a goanna dropped
down from the beam onto his bald head, round his head and
down his back. He was so bewildered, it happened so quickly.
It was hard not to laugh, I nearly choked. My mother said
afterwards, 'You never goes out except something exciting
happens.' And that was true!

We never got a smack in our lives, you know, but we were
frightened of our father. I'd make a remark at the table when
I was about fifteen. I'd say to my mother, 'Oh it's a lovely
dinner.' He'd say, 'I will not have remarks made at the table
about the food.' I said, 'I was only saying it was nice.' 'Don't
be impertinent, now my dear,' said Pater. 'Well,' I said, 'you
started it.' He said, 'Leave the table.' I'd say, 'Well, I can't

take it with me.' I just had to have the last word by that stage. And later I'd take my dinner out of the safe and eat it.

Honesty was the main thing with my father – truthfulness, you must never lie. Father never used the word 'lie'; it was a falsehood. Never tell a falsehood. To me until this day that is one of the worst sins of all: people who don't tell the truth.

I was only allowed to go teaching – that's all my father would let any of us do. Other things wouldn't do for us; all I knew of was to be a shop girl behind the counter. I don't know what else there was, but working in people's houses. That wasn't anything to do with us or our family. We were allowed to teach, or to stay at home. I don't know why teaching should be regarded as any better than charing or cleaning out someone's house, but it was.

I was twenty-six when I went into the teacher's training college. That was 1914. It's a terribly confused part of my life, I don't remember a great deal about it. As you know, to punish me, my father made me stay home. Well, by the time I was twenty-six I nearly climbed up the wall. I sat the exam I had failed ten years before and passed. I went into teachers' college for six months and then I had a country school allotted me. The six months was a special short course in the college for country teachers, mostly for pupil teachers and monitors.

When I came out I was sent to Lake Hines, a little country school with nineteen children, fourteen miles out of Wongan Hills and about 200 miles from Perth. A one teacher school – they're all gone now. But those children taught me how to teach. I didn't know children and I didn't know how to teach. I was so much above their heads, it's a wonder they understood anything at all. I should have been lecturing at the training college, not teaching little children in a country school! I found out you had to talk to a child as a child. I learned 'children' in that school – they were darlings, the nineteen of them. I learned how to teach and what children were.

Also, I was a townie – I didn't know the country and I'd

had a sheltered life. The Director of Education picked out
where you had to board, and they said, 'You will board with a
Mr and Mrs Morray a quarter of a mile from school.' So I
wrote to this Mrs Morray and said I was coming. Monday was
a holiday and there were only three trains a week –
Wednesday, Friday and Monday. My mother said, 'You'd
better go on Friday night and then you can get the school
ready to open on Tuesday.' So I wrote and I said I was
coming on the Friday's train. My mother was terribly worried,
in case these people who lived sixteen miles out of town
weren't there to meet me, for the train got in at half past three
in the morning. I said, 'We'll send a telegram on top of my
letter now, so they'll be sure to meet me.' So we sent a
telegram.

A host of us were sent to the country from college and sure
enough the train pulled in at half past three and there wasn't a
sign of a railway station. The train was six feet from the
ground, sloping away, all gravel. There'd been a thunderstorm
that night and the moon was shining on the water in pools
lying all over the place. I had a pretty new navy pleated skirt
and a silk blouse. The conductor came along and said,
'Anybody for here?' I said, 'Yes, how do I get out?' They had
dress baskets in those days, they didn't have cases, and I had
the biggest dress basket you could find with straps all over it.
The conductor said, 'Well, are you going on, or staying, miss?'
I said, 'Well, I'll have to get out.' So he lifted me out. There
was nobody there to meet me; there was no railway station,
nothing but a little corrugated iron hut and it was half past
three in the morning. I was terrified. I'd hardly been out of
the city in my life. I saw this little shanty, a corrugated iron
place. It had a hole cut – a square – in it for a window, but no
glass in it. I saw a black bearded face come to the window. I
was going to sell my life dearly, I can tell you! I sat on my
dress basket clutching my purse. This bearded man called out
'Isn't there anyone to meet you missy?' I thought, 'You'll put
poison in my tea' and 'He's a white slaver.' I'd been reading
all the melodrama – they'd laugh at me now but I was an

ingénue. I'd never had much to do except read and I used to
swallow everything I could.

Anyway there was nobody there. The train moved on and
left me there. There were no houses to go to, there was
nothing but bush and this corrugated iron place. The bearded
face looked out again and I thought, 'Oh dear, he'll murder
me.' Then he came out and said, 'If it's the Morrays, they're
always late for everything. They're sixteen miles out. I'll make
yer a cuppa tea but there's no milk and sugar until the goods
train comes tomorrow morning.' I said, 'Oh, thank you', and
sat down on my basket. He said, 'I'd ask yer in, but me mate's
in the other bed.' I thought 'Oh, goodness two of them!
What's going to happen to me?' I sat on the basket and held
my purse and remembered my new silk blouse and the
pleated skirt, oh dear. And nobody came. So he brought out a
cup of tea and when he'd gone inside I poured it into the
gravel. I wasn't going to be poisoned, I knew very well they
had ulterior motives! Then he came out again with a dirty old
rug. I was shivering with cold; it was February but they'd had
a great storm. He said, 'You'd better put this round yer or
yer'll be eaten alive with mosquitoes.' There were millions of
mosquitoes, I was like this, all the time, keeping them off.
Then he went away.

I sat upright on my basket and knew I would sell my
honour dearly. Next thing I knew, it was 7 o'clock in the
morning. I'd fallen asleep! He said 'Here's a hot cup of tea for
you, missy. Don't be frightened of us. Me and me mate have
come all the way from Queensland to do the wheat tally at all
these sidings. I've got seven kids of my own at home. You've
got no right to be left here on your own like this.' The
Morrays still didn't come at all, so this man said, 'If you like
to wait, Brownie will be along with a load of wheat to take it to
Wongan, that's fourteen miles. He'll take you into Wongan
and you can stay at the hotel until the Morrays come.' So I
said to him, 'We sent a wire and all.' He said, 'Oh, that will be
lying at the post office; they only come in once a fortnight for

mail.' So they never even had my letter, let alone the telegram!

Brownie came – he was dark burnt, like a bit of leather. He had an old hat on his head with a big hole in the crown and he was driving six horses – piled high with bags of wheat, a great big long six-wheeled affair with six horses in tandem. He came at 10 o'clock and he made a nest in the wheat. It was very hot and I couldn't keep awake.

I arrived in grand style in Wongan Hills sound asleep with Brownie holding my parasol over me and driving with one hand. He said, 'Wake up miss, it's Wongan.' We got there at 1 o'clock – all those hours to do so few miles, but the big load was heavy. He said, 'You'll get a cuppa tea at the hotel and the Morrays might be out by then.' The girl at the hotel said, 'Dinner's off. You're too late.' I said, 'I don't want anything but a bed. Just give me a bed and I'll go to sleep.' I went to get onto a bed to sleep and I said 'If a gentleman calls for me, come and wake me.' She came at 5 o'clock and said, 'A gentleman's called for you.' She had a bit of a twinkle in her eye. I said, 'Oh, where are my things?' I grabbed my hat and went out. There was this well-dressed fellow; he had on a nice navy suit and a felt hat and new tan shoes and his hair all slicked down. I said, 'Are you Mr Morray?' He said, 'No, I'm Brownie. I brought you in this morning.' He'd been home and had a bath and put on his best clothes. 'I'll take you out to Morrays,' he said. 'It's sixteen miles, the boss lent me his sulky.' 'Oh,' I said, 'Isn't that wonderful of you!' So I got up in his sulky and he put my luggage on at the back and off we went. We got to the Morrays at 7 o'clock at night, just at dusk. I was nearly dead on my feet because I used to sleep like a top when I was young.

Mrs Morray said, 'We didn't expect the teacher till Tuesday. Whenever it's a holiday she usually doesn't come till the Tuesday train.' I said, 'Oh, but the school opens on Tuesday.' She said, 'That wouldn't matter, the kids all know. The last teacher never used to come until Tuesday. She opened the

173

school a day late.' Oh, I nearly collapsed – the idea of breaking the rules! We'd been brought up to obey all the rules you know. Then she said, 'We're not ready for you – we're going to build your room tomorrow.' So I sat up nearly all night and sewed wheat bags together and they lined one end of the front verandah with wheat bags and they put a little two foot six bed in it. There was just room for my basket and me to get in. After I sewed all the bags, he nailed them up and I had a bag and safety pin for a doorway. And that was my room for 30s a week!

I lay down and went to bed, I was so worn out. I woke up and something was biting me and I was itching all over. I had a hurricane lantern – that's all I had for light – and I found there were thousands of little black beetles with a red stripe down their back. They were on my chest, on the walls – the walls of course were only made of wheat bags you know, and they were whitewashed. (This is what I came to, from a beautiful home in Perth!) I was terribly frightened and shy – one of the shyest people you ever met in those days. But I went and knocked up Mrs Morray and I said, 'Mrs Morray, there's things biting me all over.' She said, 'Oh yes, the redbacks. That's because it's damp, they like damp walls.'

Talk about the misery I suffered in this place. That's what you got for going out to be a country teacher! Mrs Morray was a religious maniac and she had an organ, a harmonium. It was up against the wall and the wall was only made of bags; and I was the other side. She'd be playing 'Nearer my God to Thee' at half past one in the mornings, with it drumming into my ears. She couldn't sleep so she'd come and play hymns.

I never was so unhappy, not all my life as I was that first year. My mother kept me alive by sending me tins of biscuits, because Mrs Morray used to stay in bed in the morning. Her girl aged fifteen was supposed to make the bread. But she'd forget to set the dough the night before, so half the time we had scones as hard and tough as anything, made in the frying pan.

There was practically no social life at all, especially at the house of the religious mania woman. I had a boyfriend, Stan, at the Front, but I also had a friend who was in the neighbourhood, he attached himself to me. He was the son of the farmer a mile past Morrays. There was nothing in it – Stan was my boy – but this local boy used to call for me on Sunday and take me for a drive in the sulky. Once he took me and his little sister to a dance held in Wongan. I can remember that they had a chalk-line drawn half way across the hall. The silver-tails danced this end and the common people danced the other side of the white chalk-line. That's an absolute fact – I'd never known such a thing before. The banker's wife said to me, 'We couldn't possibly have them up this end, men working for you, the labourers. One can't have them dancing with one.'

A man came up to me at the dance and said, 'Brownie wants to see you.' At first I said, 'Who's Brownie?' This was some months after I'd gone there. He said, 'He took you out to Morrays.' I said, 'Oh yes, I remember.' So I had to go outside to see Brownie as he was the other side of the line. Do you know what? When he took me out to Morrays that day they never even gave him a cup of tea. No refreshment: I thought country people were generous but Mr Morray came from Kalgoorlie – he was a lawyer's clerk and she thought she was a lady. So Brownie had that long drive, thirty miles in and out without anything to drink. And when Brownie went back to town that night, the horse went over a log and he was thrown out and broke his leg. He had to lie there in the bush for seven hours before someone came along. And I found all this out *months* later! I said, 'Why didn't someone tell me?' He said, 'I thought you must have known and you didn't care.' I said, 'I *do* care *terribly* and I'm sorry about it. You took me all that way, you should be paid for it.' So later I got him paid £6 from the Education Department for taking me out to the school.

As I say they had a distinct line drawn in the hall for any dancing or any social affair. There was class distinction then, I can tell you. Jack wasn't as good as his master in those days.

After a year at the country school, I took over a class in Perth with sixty children. The headmaster came in on my first day and said, 'Stand up Willy . . . Brian . . . Tom.' Five boys stood up. 'Now Miss, these are the bad eggs in the class. Any nonsense from them, send them to me and I'll trounce them.' Well, I turned to stone. I'd been teaching a year and I never thought anyone could ever be like that with children. He went out and I said, 'Boys. Sit down. I don't know your names. I don't know anything about you. Remember, everybody in this class, I love everyone of you and I hope you're going to love me.' They all said, 'Yes, miss.'

The headmaster met me a few weeks after in the passage and he said, 'Willy so-and-so has never been up for the stick. I used to cane him every day.' I said, 'But he's one of my best boys.' 'One of your best boys?' he said. 'He spent half his life out on the woodheap there. The teacher would say "Get away, get out and stay out."' I said, 'But they never learn anything if they do that.' 'Oh,' he said, 'he's a bad egg.' And what had I done when I found he had such a bad opinion of Willy? I'd said to the class, 'I want a boy I can trust. A boy to keep my cupboard tidy. I'm so untidy I don't put my books back nicely. Now who would like to be my cupboard monitor?' Every hand shot up and I said, 'Well, Willy, could you look after my cupboard?' He said, 'Yes, miss,' in a deep bass voice like a man; he was a funny little boy, about ten I suppose. But I had no trouble with him, no trouble at all.

I never believed any good came out of striking a child, not at home or at school. I don't ever remember getting a smack at home and there were seven of us. We were frightened of my father, we feared him because he was very strict. When he was an old man, eighty-four, he was staying with me just before he died and he said, 'None of you children ever loved me.' I said, 'Pater, you wouldn't *let* us love you, we were so afraid of you. You were so very stern and strict.' Our mother was so different, so loving and lovely. I said, 'But I love you now, I love you very much indeed.' He said, 'Thank you, my dear.'

I taught until I was sixty and I never struck a child. I never went round with a ruler and hit them on the knuckles or anything, I couldn't bear to hurt a child. And the children, they were always so lovely in my classes – they never misbehaved. When I was teaching, the only time I ever sent a child out for punishment was when he told a lie. I saw red, I can't stand a liar. I sent him up for the cane from the headmaster. The headmaster was too busy to cane him so he sent the boy back with the cane in his hand, with a message, 'The head said you were to cane me.' Well, when it came to the point, I couldn't do it, I couldn't hit a child, I couldn't. And so I put the cane on the table and I said, 'You sit down and behave yourself.' I couldn't do it!

There were three wars I remember during my life. The Boer War was when I was at school. My mother wrote a note to the teacher and suggested the children bring a penny a day for the patriotic fund. So they sent a note around. My mother made a calico bag with a drawstring and I went every day with the pupil teacher and gathered up all the pennies, week in, week out while the war was on. We got a considerable sum for the patriotic fund. No, we didn't feel that war was very close to us, but we were intensely patriotic! I can remember singing 'Put a Shilling in the Hat.' We went off to wave good-bye to the soldiers at the wharf before they embarked. There was no one from our family in that war but there were many young men from W.A. in that war.

The second war was quite different. The second war was the Great War 1914–1918 and I was teaching by this time. In West Australia we were very patriotic about England partly because we were the last to join the Australian federation. This war was different, we had no men left. If a man had two good legs he went off to war.

The women were pleased for their men to go. We used to have dances, the girls all danced with one another. I went to one freak dance, dressed as a soldier. I wore my brother's khaki cadet uniform, it just fitted me beautifully. The women worked hard for that war. They had all sorts of events to pay for the war. Everything was for the war. They had great bridge parties, with about ten or twelve tables about fifty playing at once. You paid so much, 2s or 5s to go and a little bit was taken out to make a prize. And we all used to take a plate. I can remember a Pommy girl being there. I said, 'Are you coming to the dance?' She said, 'What's the plate for?' She thought you had to take a plate, but I said, 'It's the food, sandwiches or cakes or whatever you've got. It's to help so you don't spend any money on the supper, it all goes to the war fund.' I never heard the expression 'Bring a plate' before that war.

We took a serious view of the war in those days. I had a boy at the war, Stan. Before he went away he was five months getting this battalion going; my young brother Rupert, who was eighteen was in it too. So when the battalion got to Egypt, they were five months training and then they were shipped off to the trenches in France. On the first moonlight night, they had orders to come out of the trenches and the Germans had a trench only thirty yards from them, ninety feet away. The moment they popped their heads up, they got the machine gun. Many lost their lives just through the proximity of the Germans. Stan only lasted half an hour and he caught a bomb. There was nothing to bury, it just blew him to pieces.

I wrote to Stan every week. The only way we got news of the First World War was by the casualty lists in the morning newspaper. There was no other way of getting news of your loved one. They gave a casualty list in the daily paper every day and I can tell you it was a long one. If someone was killed, the minister used to go to the house and break the news. Everybody got to hate the sight of a minister because they never knew if he was walking up to your house or the neighbour's. You couldn't do anything about it, they just didn't have the news facilities in those days. At that time I was teaching at my country school. Although I used to write every week and so did he, sometimes I'd get nine or ten letters in a bundle and then nothing for two or three months, because they had no way of getting letters out regularly.

In my last letter to Stan, I went out in the school ground

and pulled a gum leaf off the tree and I put the gum leaf in with my letter. I posted it in the khaki envelopes we used with their battalion number and details all in print. Then one day my landlady came down after school in a sulky. She said, 'I thought you'd like a little drive before you go home.' So we set off trotting in the sulky. She put her hand on me and said, 'I'm afraid I've got some bad news for you. It's Stan.' I said, 'Is he wounded?' She looked at me and said, 'Worse than that my dear, he's gone.' She had just got the paper that day and there was the casualty list – that's how we got the news. And his name was there, 'Killed in Action'. She had just got the paper and she'd kept it from me you see – it was a paper a week old by the time it got to the country. And my last letter to Stan came back stamped all over 'Killed in Action, Killed in Action'. Look, it would have torn you to pieces to see it. And I kept that envelope up to a year ago; I had that all these years until I came into this hospital.

I can remember the misery I felt. That was a Friday afternoon and on Saturday morning I got up and I went into the bush and I walked and walked in the bush – I don't know where I went – crying my heart out. Looking back now, it seems so silly, it couldn't do any good, crying. Then I sat down under a tree and I just sobbed. I was away all afternoon and they got worried and sent people to look for me. It was a terrible shock, you always think it can't possibly happen to you and yet it did. There was his name: 'Killed in Action'. The wounded ones were listed underneath and it said what hospital they were in.

Nobody went into public mourning for anyone killed, no black bands on your arm or anything like that. We never knew which way the war was going, we were so far away, remember that. We only knew that our men were going and not coming back. There wasn't a young man able to fight left in W.A., I'll swear to that. And if there was a young fellow with flat feet or something that they wouldn't accept, people would send him a white feather.

And he couldn't defend himself; girls used to send white

feathers too – reckoned they were cowards. I knew one young man it happened to, he not only had flat feet but no muscles either. He could walk around all right, but he couldn't have marched a mile, he would have collapsed. It was very cruel – he got a white feather – some silly little fool of a girl.

They were hard days, what with your sadness and misery about your boys at the front. And the rations – we were all rationed on food. We were a federated state and we had to do what Canberra told us. Everybody had to be rationed. It seems to me like a dream now. I was very fond of butter, we were rationed for 4 ounces a week each. We were rationed with meat and with sugar too – that didn't worry me. I used to give all my sugar coupons to somebody who made jam and they'd give me their butter ones. You were not supposed to do it – that was one of the rules; but we had to do it, we used to exchange the coupons. They wouldn't take a cut-out coupon in the shops, you had to take it out in front of them. If you lost your ration book, it was terrible trouble to get another.

With a war on like that, supplies were stopped everywhere partly because there was fighting everywhere. France was involved up to her neck and of course Germany was advancing, she'd gone through Belgium and she was advancing.

The war was the first time Australians had a part. The Boer War, when I was at school, was over my head. We used to collect funds for the soldiers, but it didn't hit home like the second war, the real world war. We must have sent a million men out of Australia easily. It was a very dreadful experience. Thousands of Australians lay in cemeteries in France.

They were long, sad, weary years. For seven years I never looked at anybody. I went on teaching and didn't take any interest in anybody and I didn't want to do anything. Then I suddenly came to life. I picked up social activities again and became dancing-mad. I met a man who was a marvellous dancer. He had come back from the war; he went on the same boat as Stan, but they didn't know each other. He came back with my brother which is how I met him. He was in London on leave during the war. They had a great big dance competition and he and an English girl won the competition waltzing from 200 couples. You couldn't go wrong when you were dancing with him, he was marvellous the way he used to handle you. Well, I married him but not for some years. He was gassed at the war; he was well when we married but the winters affected him – his lungs never got right. I lost him when my daughter was two and I went back to teaching. That was about 1923. I'm afraid my little girl had to bring herself up, much to my sorrow. She got to be too sophisticated deciding what she would wear, when she would come home from school. She used to get around me dreadfully. So apart from a three-year break when I married and had my daughter, I taught nearly all my life until I retired when I was sixty.

I think I was born too soon. I was at the tail-end of the Victorian era and too early for the twenties you might say. Things were so different in those days. We were so busy fighting for freedom from restrictions in the family – it was hard to keep our heads above water. Otherwise our father and mother would have had us nonentities. It was fighting against the parents' rule over children. They've swung to the opposite way now – the child rules the family. In those days children couldn't speak until they were spoken to: I was brought up on all that. Of course, it didn't keep me quiet. It was a battle between the old generation and the new one. And I'm not sure who won!

Now I'm over ninety. I came into hospital this past year, it's very different of course. I can't read now, to my great sorrow. My only daughter lives 600 miles from Perth. One of my best friends now to this day is Eva – I taught her as a desperately shy little girl in my first country school. She's never forgotten me and I wrote to her only this week. She lives at Albany now and I go down there to stay almost every year. But I don't think I can this year – I can't walk now. I could get there all right, I could go by plane. But I'm not putting myself on to people when I can't walk, I'm too much of a bother.

. . .

But the making of magistrates now all the rage is
And every flockmaster's a justice of peace
They find it so easy to cancel the wages
The law is their own and they rob who they please . . .

From 'Paddy's letter', collected
by A.B. Patterson

Aboriginal prisoners returning home by ship, probably about 1915

She was born on Rottnest Island in 1900, two hundred years after its discovery by the Dutch explorer, Willem de Vlaming, in 1696. Vlaming was intrigued by the small rat-like marsupials living there and named the island 'Rattsnest'. After the British settlement was founded at Swan River in 1829, the fate of the unoccupied island, nineteen kilometres from the mainland, became of interest to the settlers. Offshore islands attract attention from leisured elites as well as prison administrators and both groups decided to use Rottnest. A prison was established in 1841 to incarcerate Aboriginal men from the north, mostly for cattle-stealing offences, and the imperial governor established his summer residence on the island. While the governor's party shot wild birds and the rat-like marsupials known as quokkas, trusted inmates from the native prison acted as local gamekeepers.

The magistrate was appointed superintendent of the native prison on the island in 1898. Several inquiries into the conduct of the prison before he took up his post suggested that Rottnest was no holiday camp. For instance, in 1894 a Commission reported that prisoners were kept in chains. Disease killed large numbers. Clothes and cells were unwashed and the only vegetables on the island – carrots – were the perquisite of the superintendent's horses. There was confusion about who was sentenced for what, owing to the practice of prisoners exchanging identity bracelets.

Despite this, the magistrate's daughter spent an idyllic early childhood at Rottnest, happily protected from the knowledge of this harsh history. Three years after her birth, the native prison was closed and in 1905 her family returned to the mainland and the magistrate retired.

The magistrate had come to Australia as a young man and had married the daughter of a family who had arrived in the colony in 1830. Both came from English county families. Today, daguerreotypes of their relatives – squires and ladies – peer at the visitor, but neither the magistrate nor his wife travelled to England after retirement. Nor has their daughter visited her English relatives; after her parents' deaths, she opened a tea-room in Perth and then took in boarders.

Latterly Rottnest has become a holiday island again. Few current visitors would want to be reminded of the details of its grim history. It is several years since the magistrate's daughter last went to the island. She lives alone in the family home on the mainland, surrounded by family photographs and other memorabilia of her beloved island.

I was born in 1900 in the middle of a storm at Rottnest. The doctor couldn't get across from Fremantle and a warder's wife helped deliver me. I was the youngest. Mother brought up nine living children, having lost several babies up north. Most confinements were at home then; there was usually an old lady living around about who used to come in for the event.

My parents lived up in the nor' west before I was born. Then when my father left Wyndham, he was sent to Rottnest as superintendent of the island, when the native prison was there. He was a government servant. I can't tell you much about my father's past. He was a resident magistrate at places up in the nor' west. He wasn't a lawyer; I think they just used to pick out the sterling citizens. For petty problems, he would have a little court and deal with offenders. Then the judge would do a circuit and people the resident magistrate couldn't cope with were popped in jail until he came.

Father was a very upright man – black was black and white was white. He had to be stern – he was a magistrate. But when he wasn't on the job, he could relax and he'd be a most delightful person.

My mother was amazing. She married and went up to the north when she was very young. She was smaller than me and she was adorable – everybody loved her. All these young men used to come out from England, hoping to make their fortune and they used to come along to my parents' house and she mothered the lot of them. I don't know how she managed; she would have a bit of help, but just what was available. You just think, nine children and all these people arriving and she'd have to turn on a meal at the drop of a hat. There were times when she had a cook. I remember she had a Chinese cook: he spent his spare time cleaning the floor and when she walked into the kitchen, he used to walk after her and sweep up. So she had help when she could get it, but there were times when she couldn't.

The mothers had to bring the children up then; they didn't have nurses available. And the men had to work hard; they had no time to play around with children. Everyone in the family was very fond of Father, but he wouldn't spend time with the children like fathers do now. He appeared for meals and things, but that was it.

At Rottnest, apart from the prison, there were ordinary citizens as well. A pilot would meet the boats, there were fishermen and then there were warders of the prison. These people all had wives and children, so there was a school. The little building they used to use as a school is still there –school cum church cum hall cum everything. I think they did baking at the prison. Apart from that, everything was sent over once a week by two little boats, *Lady Forrest* and *Penguin*. The doctor used to come over every week from Fremantle to check the prisoners.

My mother was expected to entertain any celebrities who were brought over and they used to come up wide, stone steps to our house from the shore. The houses were all built from the lime-stone in a local quarry. Mother used to turn on an amazing meal. She had two unmarried grown up daughters. There were some nice old prisoners and they used to come to hew the wood and draw the water and do the fetching and carrying. So we used to have a thoroughly good old-fashioned meal. Mother's specialty was a wonderful steam pudding with a white sauce. If we had apples we had baked apples; just a good old-fashioned home meal, like we have now. We did not go in for frills. We all sat down: Father carved. There might be Sir John Forrest and Lady Forrest and the doctor. There was usually someone from the Public Works who came over to make sure things on the island were in order. Then there was Government House: the governor and his party always came in the summer. My parents were entertained there, but I don't remember much except that Lady Lawley, the governor's wife, once had a terrific children's party.

Then there was the prison. I was terrified of the prisoners. You were frightened of any strangers but I wasn't frightened of the blacks as blacks. Father gave them an afternoon off each week and they were free to roam around on the island and do what they wanted to do. They could catch fish. At one point when black snakes were really bad, Father said he'd give them a stick of tobacco (much loved by the prisoners) if they caught snakes in their time off. If they brought them to him, he would give them a stick of tobacco. So on their free afternoon, Father would perch on a stone and the natives would come along with their snakes and Father would fork out the tobacco. Well, they are very bright, you know, the natives, and he soon discovered they were borrowing each other's snakes. So he resorted to a mean trick – he used to take a little chopping block and a tomahawk and when they brought their snakes along, he used to chop their heads off.

Only 'good conduct' prisoners were sent to Rottnest. They brought them down from the north to prison on the mainland and they weren't used to the restrictions of ordinary prison, being cooped up in cells. So selected ones were sent over to Rottnest. They did jobs; they did the work about the place, under supervision. They used to wear unbleached calico uniforms – jacket and long pants: they looked like a pair of pyjamas, marked with a broad arrow.

There are salt lakes at Rottnest and they were very

productive. The Rottnest salt was beautiful quality. I can remember old barges coming over from the mainland and salt would be bagged up and stored in the island salt-house until the barges came to take it. Beautiful salt. The prisoners used to help with that. It was fascinating in the summer, when the water in the salt lakes would evaporate and leave the dried salt. It was rocky, I used to think it was like ice. There was a little old place – there's just the rubble of it left – called the salt-house, where they'd boil the water until it evaporated and left this lovely salt, very white.

When I was five my father retired and we came back to live in Perth. I went to Perth College, the up-and-coming school. Those Perth College sisters were highly educated English women and they gave up their lives for us. They taught us to live up to high ideals. The ideal was to turn out good citizens – and they turned out good citizens. I think we were taught and encouraged to be public-spirited. We had every advantage, take it or leave it. Being sisters of the church there was a religious background – we always started the day with a prayer and a hymn, a very good start for children, it gets them thinking a bit.

They used to concentrate on religious instruction which was a very good thing. We got a good grounding which I hope made better people of us. The sisters started with the idea of a school where country girls could be educated. I don't think their fees were exorbitant, not as school fees are now, and the sisters were always prepared to help where they felt it was necessary. There was not a great number of families at the school then, as Perth was a small community.

When I left school, I knew my fate. I had very old parents so I had to stay at home. But my mother didn't believe in girls just leaving school and being idle, so she plunged me into voluntary work. Anything and everything. I used to do church work: the archbishop's wife started what was called the Girls' Lunch Club. She found so many of these youngsters wandering around at lunch-time, with nowhere to go to have lunch. Girls from offices and shops used to go. There was a

huge room where we used to put a white cloth on trestle
tables and she used to have vases of flowers. The girls would
come in at twelve and eat their sandwiches. There was a huge
tea urn at the end of the room; we'd put cups and saucers out
and these girls would come and buy a cup of tea for one
penny, twopence for cocoa or coffee. An old lady, a paid
helper, attended to the gas jets; she kept the water boiling and
did the washing up afterwards. We used to help out and dry
up. The girls had their lunch and cup of tea and went.
Otherwise they were just roaming round Perth aimlessly for
an hour or so, nothing to do, dragging their feet, looking
tired. The archbishop's wife thought they needed a proper rest
and a cup of tea. And they appreciated the lunch room, a lot
of them used it.

Then the '14 – '18 war came, so then there was war work.
The base hospital for the troops was started down at
Fremantle. We joined V.A.D., Voluntary Aid Detachment. We
wore a long holland frock, seven inches from the ground and
a white nurses' apron, with V.A.D. on the front. Some used to
go every day, but I had other commitments; I used to go on
Friday afternoon. We used to go past the sentry at the hospital
with our little passes. The hospital provided a meal for these
poor men and our job was to wait on them. They –
convalescents – sat at long trestles on benches. Then we'd
clear all that up and then at 5 o'clock, they would have their
tea in great china mugs. Normally, they would have bread and
jam, but the V.A.D.s decided to supplement hospital fare, with
sausage rolls, or cakes, and we'd cut up salads greens. We'd
tidy up after that lot and then we'd run like anything to catch
the train from Fremantle to Perth at six. We'd get home at
seven, change into a ball frock, sometimes go up to Guildford
(on the train for cars were very few and far between).
Guildford was *the* place for dances: we had a gorgeous dance
and a lovely supper. More often than not, we caught the very
last train home. If we caught the very last train, we didn't
connect with the tram, so after all that day we used to walk
home two or three miles in our balldresses. How we did it

after the ordeal at the hospital I don't know; but we were so healthy.

We had to travel in groups: you wouldn't tackle a two- to three-mile walk on your own at night. Our parents wouldn't let us go unless there was a man of some description with us. It was quite different then. We used to travel in packs and love it. People belonged to church groups, we'd go to hockey matches in crowds and play badminton at nights. No pairing off. You did lead a communal life, you were all in it together.

At home, my father was ill. We didn't have help. We had to do the household chores, the shopping and the washing up and I made most of my own clothes. I would have liked to have gone to the university but my parents were very old and I was needed at home. People looked after their old families then −it was your job and that was that. You didn't resent it, it was just your job.

And there you have the story of my wicked life! But I don't seem to have wasted much time. I don't think I've done too badly.

Newnham College, Cambridge (the class of 1910) – the
bishop's daughter is second from right in the second row
from top

Tangmalangaloo

The bishop sat in lordly state and purple cap sublime,
And galvanized the old bush church at Confirmation time;
And all the kids were mustered up from fifty miles around,
With Sunday clothes, and staring eyes, and ignorance profound.
. . .

'Come, tell me, boy,' his lordship said in crushing tones severe,
'Come, tell me why is Christmas Day the greatest of the year?
How is it that around the world we celebrate that day
And send a name upon a card to those who're far away?
. . .

A squall of knowledge hit the lad from Tangmalangaloo.
. . .

The ready answer bared a fact no bishop ever knew —
'It's the day before the races out at Tangmalangaloo.'

– P.J. Hartigan ('John O'Brien')

Riding side-saddle in Kings Park, Perth, 1906

Born in England in 1887, she arrived in Australia when she was eight years old. Her memories are about the ways in which values were transferred from English upper-middle-class society to Australia. Her story illuminates some of the colonial ballads of the period, which describe the collision between stereotypes, the 'Bai Jove' Englishman (lisping, effete and bored) and his colonial cousin (straightforward, frank and democratic). For example, Henry Lawson's 'Ballad of Mabel Clare' describes Mabel, the democratic daughter of a cockatoo out west who had a 'manly independence' and who hated 'swells and shining lights'. But she betrayed her origins by marrying a swell with an 'eye glass to his eye, and a collar to his ears', and as well, a mouth 'formed for sneers.' But after Mabel married Lord Kawlinee, he revealed himself to be a true Australian rouseabout, instead of a member of the English upper crust, so all was well. But the point was that the literature of the time said clearly:

> There's nothing so exasperates a true Australian youth
> Whatever be his rank in life, be he cultured, or uncouth
> As the manner of a London swell . . .

These views must have induced a tension between the church, as most of the clergy of the time were English, and potential parishioners. Nineteenth-century English novelists indicate that being a gentleman was an essential part of being a priest. Indeed, there is Thomas Hardy's rather acid comment:

To succeed in the Church, people must believe in you, first of all, as a gentleman, secondly, as a man of means, thirdly as a scholar, fourthly as a preacher, fifthly, perhaps, as a Christian – but always first as a gentleman.

195

In ballads of the bush, the clergyman or priest is a surprisingly prominent figure, although there is little poetic record of the women of the church, the nuns or the deaconesses. The ballads see the main functions of these poetic priests as ceremonial – christenings, marriages and funerals – rather than spiritual. The bushman's main source of spiritual communion seemed to be with the stars.

Although the bishop of this story was an English priest, he managed to escape censure as a 'swell' in the colony, perhaps as his daughter suggests, because of his direct north country manner. Most of the women in this book from the stockrider's daughter to the magistrate's daughter knew him and admired him.

The bishop's daughter was brought up in Perth. As a young woman, she made two visits to England, once to go to University at Cambridge. For most of her subsequent life, she has stayed at home, and has undertaken a certain amount of voluntary work, such as organizing a patients' library in a hospital.

A year ago she was moved to a nursing home from her flat, because her walking deteriorated and her vision is poor. But she is not ill and she has her own room and tries to keep busy by knitting and reading books with large print. Most of her own generation have died and she has few visitors. She remembers a past which is based on the values of propriety and precedence and recounts her mainly pleasant memories in a discursive way.

I was born at Preston in Lancashire, my father was vicar of a Parish there: that's partly why I got the name of Pauline as one of my names. St Paul was a rugged sort of a nature, I suppose, and so was my father. He had a rugged sort of a nature and way of talking, and a carrying voice. He could be heard in the cathedral without sounding boards.

My father's father was a clergyman. Have you read *Cranford?* Well, Cranford is Knutsford where my mother was born, in Cheshire I think. My father's father was Vicar of St Cross Church in Knutsford, and Knutsford was Cranford. A lot of

Cranford remained much the same when I was in England in 1907. A street with several elderly ladies, including my father's only sister, in a row of cottages, with a little maid each. My aunt gave her maid 5s a week and people thought that was dreadful. *But* there wasn't much to spend money on. They didn't have evenings off, they had afternoons off. They might have social afternoons and so on, but nothing expensive, and you could buy a blouse then for one eleven three, [1/11¾] as they called it and things were cheap. And maids got all their food, you see. They had the same food as we did; their main meals were at the mistress's expense. So it sounds poverty stricken, but it wasn't as bad as it sounds. One maiden lady or a widow each had their own little maid. Three in a row, friends, in Cranford Avenue.

My father was born in Birmingham, but his father came to this church in Knutsford when he was young. Then I think he went to Manchester Grammar School, but that I can't be positive about. Then I think he went to what was called Owen's School in Manchester and from there, he got a scholarship to go to Caius College, in Cambridge.

After Cambridge my father was at a church in Yorkshire. I don't know how many curacies he had, but the one we used to hear about was with a certain Canon Edwards who was the rector. (The said Canon Edwards' daughter married a clergyman and came out here to Perth as rector of a church. The said Canon Edwards christened me and their daughter is my godchild. She lives in England and she's still alive; I got a letter from her last Christmas.)

I don't know if my father's church at Preston was a 'living'. Lots of 'livings' were in the gift of the lord of the manor, but I never heard of the church at Preston being this. You see Preston was a manufacturing town. Horrockses Mills were there – they made sheeting and towels. Horrockses calico was noted as being good – it was a good mill. Most of the parish were mill people. It was quite a working-class parish. Just a few better-class people in it and more on the border. I mean, there would be a doctor and the headmistress of what we would call a state school. There was one we knew quite well.

She was a better-class woman herself, but the children she had to teach were rougher. My father got on very well with people in the parish, that's what helped to make him popular later, in Western Australia. This was one instance. He was going up to one of the country places and a sleeper had evidently been booked for him on one of the night trains, but also one had been booked for the Roman Catholic bishop and the rail people had mixed them up. The Roman bishop arrived first and was given his sleeper. Then father arrived and there was no seat for him. So workmen in one of the compartments said, 'Never mind, Bishop. Come in here, there's room in here for you. We've got some tucker.' I don't *think* they presumed; he could keep his own position and they respected him, but yet . . . there was this north country manner.

Bishop Parry, the second bishop, here, had died and I think that those instrumental in getting my father out here thought that a rugged man like him would be a good one. You see the gold-rush had just started, and there were a terrible lot of miners and things about, all on the goldfields. This is only by the way, but mother said that after my youngest brother was born she had one miscarriage. She was a strong woman, but she said she supposed it was partly the shock of suddenly having to come out such a long way. It was much more of a business than it is now.

My mother's people were not county, my mother's father was just a country doctor. Well educated, but he had eleven children, so he hadn't money to send them to college. Mother wasn't a student at all, but she could learn a language, she was quite good at French. She didn't know much else. Being a country doctor's daughter she was better at driving a sulky, which she much preferred to lessons. She was a tomboy. Well, she had six brothers, what can you expect? And she was one of the younger girls.

I was nearly eight when we landed in Australia in 1895. It took us seven weeks to come. We went to Bishop's House; it had not been occupied by Bishop Parry latterly, because he just couldn't afford to keep it up, the income was quite small in those days. It was increased soon after father came. With the gold-rush and things, there was an influx of people and people were arriving in large numbers.

We lived in Bishop's House until father died in 1929. It was added onto, of course. It was just like an English vicarage I suppose. It had fireplaces in all the downstairs rooms and one or two rooms had circular grates, you could put a kettle on the edge; there was a biggish oven for coal or wood, a two-sided one so you could have things hot or tepid, as you wished.

In one way we did a certain amount of entertaining, but we didn't have very big functions. We had a cook and a house parlourmaid and we brought our own nurse with us. She stayed until my sister was two and then got married. Then we had what was known as a lady help – a friend who came and looked after the baby and the younger ones. Then we had a governess. You've probably heard of Sir Walter and Lady James. They came from Carmarthen in South Wales. Well, our governess was Lady James' younger sister. She was a Welsh woman, not very old (only seventeen or eighteen, although we didn't realize that – she looked older) and she'd come out to visit them. Then we also had a sort of gardener and we had a cow – most people had a cow then. Gradually we gave up having a cow and got a milkman.

A bishop's wife doesn't have the same sort of visiting as a priest's wife does, but my mother had to go to more functions and things. And then, as I say, when the nurse married, another girl, who was a friend really, came and lived with us. She was one of the old families, but she had no money, so she had to do something, so her mother and grandmother were pleased that she should come into a gentleman's household. She lived with us – she didn't have her meals in the kitchen, she had her meals in the dining-room, like the governess would. Of course, when the children were smaller, when the youngest ones still had to have their meals in the nursery, she would have her main meals in the nursery with them. We all had them there until we were a respectable age to behave properly at table.

We had no car until 1924. We had a pony and trap, what

199

they called the phaeton, same sort of thing as the landau, but
a poor relation. Two seats facing each other. You had to
have a strongish pony. Mother, being a country doctor's
daughter, had learned to drive, luckily. We had to have a trap,
as father was always having to catch trains and go to meetings.
When he was away, of course, mother used to drive us about.
What I meant about strength was that steepish hills in the park
could be quite an effort for a pony.

I was twelve when I first went to school – I went to a small
private school. Children of our sort of class did not go to state
schools in those days. None of us went to a state school; I'm
not sure whether any of my nephews and nieces did, but in
my own generation I only knew of one lot amongst our
friends who went to state school. There were three boys – they
went to state school, but it was marked that their manners and
so on were a bit different to the other boys. Oh, they mixed
with us, and we didn't *despise* them because they'd been to
state school, but there was a difference then. I don't think
you'd notice it so much now, they have better teachers now, I
think.

There were plenty of children in your own class and your
own school and you didn't mix up with the others and the
houses weren't so mixed up, anyway. Now it's more a case of
whether you can afford the houses, I think. Then, you could
have social position and still have very little money.

Clergy always had a social position of sorts and they're
naturally of various classes, apart from whatever denomination
they belong to. They have to have a certain amount of
education. But with them, it does make a difference whether
they've been to private school, or not. If they have, it gives
them, the ones that went to private school, easier manners. If
you understand what I mean, they find it easier to mix with all
classes than the ones one would call lower class, who are more
brash. My father was the same manner with whoever he met,
unless perhaps he happened to be talking to royalty (naturally
you have to use certain terms when you're speaking to them).
But ordinarily, you'd treat any older person much the same in

whatever class they were – not like the youngsters do now. They don't seem to worry how old you are, I notice that with the younger nurses and so on, here.

Mother was very strict. Although it was quite harmless, I wasn't allowed to go into town by myself until I was eighteen. I took care to put my hair up the day I was eighteen (I had long hair down to my waist). She'd seen some girls of our own class coming back from school and didn't think they were behaving very nicely with each other. But I think it was probably quite harmless: I might bicycle to the hockey club but she didn't like me going shopping in town, for some reason, until I got my hair up.

The hockey was started by some girls who'd come from here; they started it when they came back having played it at boarding school in England. Girls over fourteen could come, but they expected them to be a better class of girls, not just anyone.

We weren't allowed to think ourselves anybody because we were the archbishop's children or anything, but still, you met everybody all the time. When I was a growing-up girl, it was taken for granted, as the bishop's daughter, that we would be at all functions and everything. There was no fuss about it and no fuss about dress. Apropos of clothes and the way they now will want so many – in here they want you to wear a different frock each day – we had one new winter best suit or dress, which would appear at all the things we went to, in the day-time and one special new evening frock. But the *last* year's one would then do for all the subscription dances. And yet, I suppose we had just as much money in a way and with maids, we had more time to make them. I made a lot of my own things. It didn't worry us about dress, we knew what we were going to wear and wore it. In those days things were much simpler than they are now.

My father was keen on girls being educated, but I was the only one of the three girls in the family who went to a university. Two out of the three boys did. In 1907 when I was twenty I went to Cambridge, to Newnham College.

Cambridge is the family university. My father's father was a Cambridge man and my father was Cambridge and my eldest brother too. My brother went there the year before me – he got a government scholarship. I didn't get a scholarship, but it only cost £30.00 a term to be at Newnham and that meant board and lodging and washing all your linen and everything (you paid for your private washing). But the tuition came out of that, so it wasn't expensive at all.

There weren't so many from here at Cambridge then, but there were two women's colleges, Newnham and Girton. Newnham had 150-odd students and Girton just more . . . so English girls were going then to university.

Going to Cambridge didn't worry me as much as it may have worried some, because I had plenty of relations in England. One of them was one of the judges of the time, but they varied as to what they did. So England never struck me as very strange, but it may have done to some. There were one or two other Australian girls – do you know the Symes in Melbourne? They were sort of top dogs, weren't they, and certainly they had money, but they were educated, too. Evelyn was at Newnham the same time as I was, but she died quite a long time ago.

There were a few girls who always seemed to be more common. I don't know why it was, they came from all sorts of homes. It never struck me that there was anything strange about Cambridge except that there were one or two girls I wouldn't have made bosom friends of, because they weren't like the people I was used to. But there was nothing really wrong with them. But then, it was different for me, because I had English relations.

Mother, my sisters and my middle brother took a house in Bedford. She was in England for eighteen months or so to give the others a bit of English education. Bedford was a cheap place and you got a decent house. And it was close to Cambridge.

We went to men's lectures, unless the professor objected. I had very few lectures in college – we had tutors up there. But practically all my lectures – I was doing history – and some of the other subjects also, were the same with the men. We rode up and down to lectures on bicycles. And if you met men at lectures, you didn't know them. It was extraordinary – I mean I had a brother up there all the time I was there, because he got four years and I only got three and we left together, but I only met him about once in the street while I was there and I went to lectures twice a week at his college and I never struck him. If you had a brother, the authorities had to know it. He could come and see me at Newnham. He had to ring the doorbell, he couldn't just walk into my room, but the maids soon knew if they were your brothers or not. And you weren't supposed to have other girls in the room while he was there.

But still, he could come and see me all right, but I couldn't go to see him. On a Sunday afternoon, generally he came up to see me, and generally when it was too early to go out paying calls. You went to see his master's wife one Sunday a month and that took the whole afternoon – you weren't supposed to pay a half-hour call. She entertained the undergrads' sisters, or, I suppose, girlfriends if they really had them, and his tutor's wife or mother. And then there were one or two others who were friends of my father's – we went to see their families. So my brother could go out with me like that. And there was one cousin of my mother who was wife to the Rector of Maddingly, which was four miles out, so we used to bicycle out there. Then we rather broke the rules, because there was a friend of my brother's, who was at another college, who was also a friend of these people. He used to bicycle with us. Well, I mean it was four miles out, so it was much more sensible for two men to go than one.

In England then, I think that Mrs Pankhurst and Co. were still going around. She didn't seem as startling a person as I expected. The thing was, at Newnham, we were allowed to be suffragists, but not suffragettes, if you know the difference. The suffragettes were the noisy crowd. The suffragists were barracking all the time for the vote, but they didn't have noisy meetings or do anything violent or anything. They came and talked like any other speaker who'd come in.

But I'd say I was never interested in politics. We had a

political debating society; there were three parties and I forget
what they were. But one was liberal–unionist and I think that
some of us more colonial ones became liberal–unionists and
they said we were the 'wobblers', because we voted with either
side, according as it pleased us. But this debating society, in
my time, was carried on more or less on parliamentary lines,
once a week. It was to teach girls to speak at meetings and
things and so on. The suffrage didn't worry me in the least,
because I knew that when I came back to Australia, I had a
vote. Nobody worried about it very much out here, I don't
think. It came easily I suppose; one never heard very much
about it here. At Cambridge I went to the meetings, because it
was something to do in the evenings. We didn't go out very
much, because we had to be in by eleven. I mean, even if you
were coming back with one of the dons, you still had to be in
by eleven. The only occasion you might be out after eleven
was the Greek play, which they had once in three years – you
got one Greek play during your time. Men might be out later
but they had to pay a fine. It meant their names were put
down in the books, even though the fine was not very
expensive, twopence or something.

When we left Cambridge, we were given a certificate to
show we'd passed the necessary examinations, as women
weren't admitted to degrees in those days. I suppose some
were resentful in a way, but we knew it would come. I forget
when it came in that Oxford and Cambridge gave degrees to
women – 1925 is the date I've got in my head. After I came
out here again, the university began in 1913 here and I was
given what they called the *ad eundem* degree.

I came back to Australia in 1910 and helped my mother for
a few years. Then in 1913 I took my younger sister home. We
went on a White Star Boat because they were cheaper. The
trips were quite good and the White Star were better than the
Bay boats. For one thing they had meals at the times one was
used to. You had dinner at night, not that we had dinner at
night at home always, because being a lot of school children,
living close to school, we had our dinner occasionally in the
middle of the day. But I found the ship quite pleasant and

there generally were some quite nice people on board, even if we didn't know anyone to start with. I think when I took my sister home, another family was going home to England to school and I used to teach the two girls and my own youngest sister in the mornings in the dining saloon – well, it occupied them. Except when it was very hot and so on.

I scandalized some of the people on board ship when I was going to England. I was keen on stamp collecting and there was a Scotch doctor on board and he was quite nice and I used to discuss stamps and things with him. And some of them were scandalized because I went down to his cabin. But it was quite harmless, because his cabin was open – he left the door open always anyway. It never struck me as naughty to do it. I could see afterwards what people would mean, but there was absolutely nothing in it. We were discussing stamps and you couldn't discuss stamps in the saloon or anywhere, where there was a crowd of people. And his cabin was opposite the hospital, where there were stewards going in and out all the time. So I should think it was rather harmless, wouldn't you? The others wouldn't realize it wasn't a social sort of conversation or anything. Sometimes we would walk about on the deck together. But I mean, he was an educated man and I was an educated woman. And having been so recently at a university, you noticed the difference; the others were quite nice people, but not up to me in education, you see. (Though it didn't make any difference with the girls I grew up with.)

In England, my main interest was to see that my young sister was looked after. She was in my charge for the time being and was left mostly to stay with my aunt, and then she made friends. These friends wrote to mother – quite nice people – then she went to stay with them. That was until war began, then that upset everything. What upset my sister the most about the war was that the Army took over her school playing fields.

I returned to Australia just before war broke out and I stayed home for a good part of the first war, or both wars, for that matter. But for most of the first war, I was the only one at home. Both my sisters had got caught in England – they didn't get back until 1919, because women weren't allowed to travel. I went on various committees, I suppose. I only went onto things like serving meals and so on, where there were a lot of people and one couldn't go, as we were a maid short at home. I went to meetings and things. And I gave religious instruction in state schools. That was two mornings a week. There was a shortage of clergy, especially then, because some had gone away as chaplains.

And I kept on my work with the Perth Hospital library during the war. I didn't always go into the wards myself. For quite a while I did when we were pretty short-handed. It worked all right. We always got our own people; we didn't just take people who came into the room who said they'd like to do something – quite unsuitable people to do bookwork. The patients liked someone who would come and talk to them as well as let them choose books.

I think the idea of bluestockings, even when I went to England, had more or less been given up and it was getting to be more the thing to do for girls to go on to Cambridge or Oxford – I don't know about the provincial universities. It did depend rather on whether you got married or not, although educated women were beginning to get married. Not that I had any intention, it didn't worry me as to whether I would get married. I mean, I had men friends and so on and met them at dances, but all *that* sort of thing was different then. Most of the dances you went to were private and you were invited to them and you went whether you were invited with a man or not. You danced with the men who were there – whom you met at all the other dances you went to, probably.

As I say, my father was keen on girls being educated. It wasn't because I was brilliant, I had to work hard to get my degree. I thought if I had to earn my own living I'd be a teacher. Then the sisters had a school in St George's Cathedral and that's one of the places I taught for half a term once or twice, when teachers were sick. That was paid for, but they're the only paid jobs I've taken, I suppose. I was governess for one or two spells to Sir Gerald Strickland, the governor's children. He expected a governess to be educated. I was a graduate then and I'd been to Cambridge, where he'd also been. In those days, there were governesses and governesses: I was also a lady to look after the governor's children and it was easier for me than for others. The things the girls were invited to, I probably would have gone to anyway.

They always talk about the poor governess and so on, and governesses weren't reckoned as anything very marvellous in those days. People very often got a governess to look after the children, irrespective of their education. But my family couldn't have done that. Very few girls had jobs in those days. When my next sister got married in 1921, she was thirty. We knew so many people it would have meant having a big reception which would give her more to do, as she was the one who used to do the extra cooking and so on if we were without a cook. So we decided that we would have a morning wedding and ask the girls of the families who were about her age. Well, there seemed to be quite a biggish number there, but there were only about two girls who came to the wedding that had jobs. (They were senior in their jobs, so they could get off for an important thing like the archbishop's daughter getting married; there wouldn't be any fuss about it.)

I liked going to college and having something to fall back on. You see if you were a graduate you knew you'd get a job in those days. I suppose that prevented me worrying. I thought I'd be a teacher, I rather liked it. But it would have meant being out of the house quite a lot. And then of course with my father being bishop and archbishop here, of course, you'd mix with the Government House people and so on much more than you'd do now. I mean, one governor had children who were more or less our age and then as I said I looked after the Strickland girls.

Nursing was all right here, but I did hear that if girls went to England, they rather despised them. But I don't think they did here. My brothers married into families where there were nurses and the daughter of the Commissioner of Police became a nurse and she was a friend of ours. When father got sick she came and nursed him.

When my father died in '29, we moved from Bishop's

House to a house in Subiaco. People kindly collected money to get us a house. Then I don't know that I did anything that brought in any money after that. We weren't short enough of cash to worry about it. Of course, it was a smaller house to keep up: we only had sort of one maid and an odd gardener and didn't have a horse and trap. We still kept a car because that had been given to us about 1924; my younger sister drove it. My mother didn't die until the 1950s.

I was never terribly ambitious or anything, I never wanted to be anything special. I never thought of going into an office, I thought that would be very dull and there was income, so it wasn't necessary. Mother preferred us to stay at home and have a maid less. I suppose I was rather phlegmatic, as you might say, in a way. I didn't go out as much as a lot of girls did, even girls of my own class. We did stop at home more then. Then of course, as I got older, there were grandchildren arriving – things like that cropped up.

I always talk about England as home, still. I've never called myself an Australian. I was very fond of England but I don't want to go back, it would be too changed. I've never been back since the war. Besides, all my cousins are dead now and so are my special pals from college, except for one who lives in the Channel islands.

I don't have many visitors now; if anyone wants to take me out for a drive or anything, I'd like to go. If you think about old age too much, it's annoying, and I notice some of the others here grumble much more than I. It's difficult! I came in here fifteen months ago, not because I was ill, but because I was living in a flat by myself. But coming into hospital was not a matter of propriety, but of age and commonsense. I was not ill and I haven't been ill since being here. It is quite a contrast to come into hospital, you lose certain amenities such as the telephone. And you lose a certain freedom to go in and out as you please – you can't do as you please any longer.

She speaks

Don't you think, my dear, said my grandmother,
that I am very old? so many winters
and gifts of potted plants flowering,
so many dear children coming, from the farm,
from town, from childhoods in Australia,
to speak in my deaf ears, to wear
the faces of my sons. The four so faithful,
we went to Church together, such an old woman,
when dear Gerald was here. I used to think
it would be sinful to complain, my dear,
of being old; and then Queen Mary said
it was a perfect nuisance! if she thought
it right to say so, then perhaps I may.
My sight so bad, I cannot even read
books of the dear Queen. But the grandchildren
and kind friends often come, I am not dull,
such an old woman, yet another spring.

— Judith Rodriguez

'As for society in Australia, it is just a slice of life of Great Britain', wrote Beatrice Webb after visiting Australia in 1898. But the newcomers reproducing Great Britain in the unlikely territory of Western Australia had problems. They needed to recast their traditional British views of place and station and to set up a new social hierarchy, and this was not as easy as it sounds. First, the colonists could not consider fitting into the hierarchy established by the native population; nor could they place themselves at the top of that hierarchy and use the natives as intermediaries between the colonists and the soil, as the British did in West Africa for example. The original Australians, the Aborigines, were so alien that they were either ignored, controlled or destroyed. Second, in an isolated, deserted community, people of all conditions needed each other for economic and human reasons. Third, many of the newcomers to the colony wanted to leave behind the old traditions and habits based on class.

In spite of what individuals may have wanted, most colonial societies were based on the assumptions of conventional British (or European) social hierarchy, possible exceptions being attempts at forming ideal or utopian communities. In general, and it is not surprising, colonists were not motivated by utopian ideals and they tended to reproduce the society from where they came, because that was the form they knew best. This process took place in the Western Australian colony. But whereas in nineteenth-century Britain, most people would certainly have known 'their place' implicitly, the people eager to make a new life in the colonies were not as conscious of class delineations. For instance, the English villager, whose mind was finely tuned to the nuances of social hierarchy, would not require the chalk-line across the dance floor to mark off the 'silver-tails' from the *hoi polloi*. The accountant's daughter's description of the dances in the farming community indicates that settlers of all groups needed each other to survive, but also that these crude reminders were necessary to maintain the given social structure.

Was it possible to cross the chalk-line in colonial society? During the gold-rushes, there were many tales of fortunes made and lost and of men who went from rags to riches. But most of the women in this book have not moved significantly from their social origins. Apart from the actress, a barmaid's daughter, the tendency was for the daughters of factory workers to become factory workers themselves and to marry factory workers. There was, in fact, very little moving up or down the social scale, although materially, the lives of most of these women improved over time. Was the Victorian view that families could improve themselves socially by migration a myth? It was certainly possible to *lose* social, and financial, position in the colony, as the fate of the divorced grazier's daughter indicates. She was forced to leave her farm and live very simply after her financial ruin. For many then, perhaps the opportunities of achieving social cachet in particular in the colonies have been overstated, though the potential for a higher standard of living seems to have been better in Australia, especially for the poorer classes.

The first settlers to the colony expected to maintain their traditions through land holding. The Australian writer, Martin Boyd, makes a persuasive case in his novels for the existence of an Australian upper class at the turn of the century. His view is based on the transfer of the British ideal that a gentleman was a land owner who did not work for money, but who devoted his life to leisured cultivation of the soil, to hunting, shooting and occasional good works. In spite of the possibilities of being a land owner, only a very small elite could enjoy such a luxurious lifestyle, and most 'gentlemen' in Australia had to struggle and to work hard with their hands, and their daily activities were practically indistinguishable from *arrivistes* who rose by their own merits. The gold-rushes, providing as they did the chance for anyone to become wealthy and forcing the mixing together of all social groups, perhaps contributed to the demise of an aristocratic tradition in the colonies. The lives of some of the young women provide interesting illustrations of some of the surviving complex social rules: whom one would (or would not) invite to the dinner table; whom one would (or would not) dance with; where one would (or would not) go to school.

Although there were many similarities between the colonial society and the Britain from which the settlers had come, there were startling differences too. As the working women of this book imply, feelings of self-respect rather than inadequacy, and of independence rather than dependence, characterized the young Australian working woman. The extent to which these qualities were affirmed by the rigors of the Australian environment is difficult to say. These qualities are particularly striking when one considers that, until the twentieth century was well advanced, most women in Western Australia had to work extremely hard for the first half of their lives at least. By 1890, when the shortage of female labour was well known, women undertook back-breaking, physical work for the family, such as doing the washing by hand for large families out of doors in the heat in iron tins. As well, many women were of considerable economic importance to the family because of their contribution to the management of farms. Growing vegetables and looking after the fowls all obviated cash transactions and thus contributed substantially to the family economy. At the same time, women had to swing axes and to dig holes, thus blurring the conventional distinctions between men's and women's work.

In the towns, too, the contributions of women were just as essential to the survival of their family. Work in the house was not only a matter of maintaining rituals of hygiene and habits of household management, but also a matter of supporting the family, by making the spending of money unnecessary. Even if cash was available, it might not purchase the immediate needs of the family. At a neighbourly level, something akin to a barter system seemed to operate. One woman, the butcher's daughter, gave away goat's milk while the farmer donated fruit; another, the odd jobber's daughter, remembers a gift of glass from the French neighbours for windows. This unspecialized economy was based on exchange rather than money and locked many colonists into mutual aid, a system which has almost disappeared now, having been replaced by a society dependent on cash exchanges and material consumption.

For women who needed a job outside the home, there were limited opportunities available in such an isolated colony. Three quarters of the women employed in Western Australia in 1901 either worked in service, or in the manufacturing or sale of clothing, or in maintaining board and lodgings. A few women were employed in the embryonic public service, particularly as typists in offices, or as postmistresses and telegraphists. There were a number of teachers who were women, some of them married, and a few nurses were employed by the government service.

In her description of the limited occupations open to women at the time, the barmaid's daughter reveals one colonial preoccupation, the attention to physical attractiveness by women. Many male visitors to the colony at the time commented favourably in their memoirs on the standard of attractiveness of barmaids or maids. Dressmakers lived off female wishes for finery. Herbert Hoover, later President of the United States, worked on the Kalgoorlie goldfields as an engineer and extolled the charms of the barmaid: his 'red-lipped, sunbrowned sweetheart, dark-eyed daughter of the south'. Perhaps for a woman, outward presentability came to be seen as another mark of having crossed the chalk-line, since for most, the only way to move up the social ladder was through marriage to a man with a more prestigious occupation than her father.

Marriage was the path to social improvement, partly because of the limitations of jobs for women. Yet perhaps because the range of choices was quite restricted, many women were allowed an expressiveness within their jobs now denied women in today's more specialist society. The barmaid of 1900 could act as a social worker and a counsellor, a dressmaker was also a dress designer and a fashion consultant, a postmistress was head of the news grapevine as well as a telegraphist, a teacher was not only a pedagogue but a symbol of an educated, civilized woman. Today's specialization has decreased the number of functions performed by women at work. Perhaps it has also reduced job satisfaction.

The upper middle-class family seemed to exercise as powerful a force on the development of its members in the colonies by the end of the century as it did in Britain. Paternal authority and influence moulded the lives of the daughters of the accountant, the magistrate and the bishop. In the working-class families, the mothers, rather than the fathers, seemed to be more significant as controllers of behaviour and outlook. One aspect which contradicts expectations is the lack of physical discipline imposed by fathers in working-class families. With the exception of the timbercutter, working-class fathers were seen as benign, kind and soft hearted. One wonders if the legendary Victorian father who thrashed his offspring twice weekly was a middle-class rather than a working man, for most Victorian autobiographies and biographies come from persons from middle- and upper-class families.

The accounts of these women raise new questions about family relationships in marriage. At present, it is assumed that high rates of distress and trauma in marriage, as indicated by the current high rates of divorce, are a result of rapid social changes in the late twentieth century. But women of the previous generation, when looking back on their marriages, do not see satisfaction. Half of the women were very negative about their marriages. Three were divorced (the grazier's daughter, the butcher's daughter and the brewery worker's daughter); two others regretted their marriages bitterly (the timbercutter's daughter and the miner's daughter). Other women were more neutral and rather less critical of their marriages, but their memories were not very positive either (the clerk's daughter and the accountant's daughter).

These women, then, did not have happy and satisfying marriages. Perhaps they assess their marriages more critically now in retrospect than they did at the time because their views of what marriage might achieve have altered along with the views of the rest of the community. Women now consider personal fulfilment to be a potential goal of marriage. All except two of the women interviewed have outlived their husbands and they considered that widowhood has brought them new and relished freedom. 'For forty years, I had to have his tea on the table at 5 o'clock,' explained the miner's daughter, who became a miner's wife. 'It's marvellous, just being able to please yourself!'

The unmarried women appear to have had less difficulty adapting to old age than the married women. By and large, they have been able to sustain life-long interests and hobbies, they are less dependent on relatives for emotional support and they appear to have maintained a wider circle of friends than the married women. Of course, these observations cannot be translated into generalizations about all elderly women, as there may be biases in the selection of the women and it is a very small group. But the experiences of these women tend to confirm the present finding of psychiatric and sociological research: that marriage is better for men than for women. Married women suffer from higher rates of physical and mental ill health than single women, whereas the reverse is true for men.

Being respected was an important goal of these women, whatever their marital state, and understanding this motivation is often a key to understanding their behaviour. Being straightforward and honest and decent seemed to be regarded as genuine virtues, not as hypocritical covers for ulterior motives. Perhaps the hard environment was an influence, but, in any case, the possession of these virtues seems to remove these women and their mothers a long way from the stereotypes of vacuous Victorian British women, who behaved like simpering helpless fools, and dealt with problems, physical and environmental, by withdrawing to the chaise-longue. These women undertook hard physical work and, at times, heavy responsibility. Their accounts do not suggest that they solved their 'problems of identity' through dependence on others, whether a husband or children. Life presented them with too many difficulties that were quite literally concerned with maintaining the alternative of life as opposed to death. Food needed to be grown and prepared so that the family stayed alive; children needed to be nursed during illness so they did not die;

men needed to be fed to keep them strong so they could maintain the viability of the farm. Respectability, then, was a kind of transubstantiation, a process which could transform hard physical labour in the house or on the farm or amongst the fruit trees into a meaningful purpose.

Some writers have suggested that the 'meaningful purpose' for which women worked was to tame and then civilize the unsubdued land for family, for community and then for empire and much has been made of the fact that colonial women were invited to see their lives in terms of this cultural mission. The degree to which women had a *separate* mission from men needs further exploration. The mission of promoting the virtues of British civilization within the family seems to have been of greater consequence to the women, partly because they lived more isolated lives; this value, untainted by the economic or political pressures operating in the world of their menfolk, remained central to the women.

The exclusion from these reminiscences of political or many very personal issues is noticeable. One of the women, who lived on Rottnest Island, was totally unaware of the controversies and traumas surrounding the history of the prison there. Another, battered and assaulted in childhood, thought her experiences were unique and carried her sorrows with her into old age. A third could not relate the private pain of the loss of her fiancé in the First World War to any wider issues about this war or war in general. A fourth believed that her family had good relationships with Aboriginals – yet it was in her town at the time of her story that part-Aboriginals were first excluded from state schools, banned from the town and eventually segregated onto settlements. The mutual aid system arranged for the exchange of goods did not extend to sharing or externalizing pains and burdens: the 'sisterhood' and politicization that were the focal points of the feminism of the 1970s are foreign to these lives. Perhaps because these women rarely made any connections between their private lives and public events, they were content to allow the maintenance of the *status quo;* it was this conservatism that some historians considered influential in the decision to enfranchise Western Australian women so early.

Because so few of these strong, respectable, isolated women entered the public arena, younger Australian women tend to be ambivalent about their grandmothers' and great-grandmothers' lives. On the one hand, they reject and dismiss them as constrained, conventional women, lacking in opportunities. They hold a simple linear view of progress and consider themselves to be liberated, individualistic and enterprising. On the other hand, there is a certain intrigue about the women of the past, reflected in anthologies of women's poetry, which usually have poems about an Australian grandmother or a great-grandmother. Paradoxically, these poems usually celebrate the competence, independence, initiative and imagination of the past generation. Lee Knowles describes her grandmother in this way:

My straight-eyed grandmother
at the end of a long house like a tram,
receives friends, writes her own letters,
makes her own soup.

It was always so.
Grandmother stood, the arbiter, hard at the door.
She killed the chooks, she snapped the summer fruit,
could snap into ice my wayward cousin.

New married, she faced a wild bush farm,
and did not flinch when my unknown grandfather, encased in a hard
  shell of ideals,
revealed the burning pit in his head,
that caused him such strange pain.

It grew, and she took over.

Grandmother took her babies in a basket
into the sun-fierce paddock. She grew pumpkins of amazing girth,
learnt not to listen to the night wind's secrets.

My unknown grandfather
was carried into the kitchen,
the fire at last gone from his skull,
the space clean.

She mopped up the mess, sold the farm, and went on
to set her living children on their way.

Now she sits,
my straight-eyed grandmother,
where she always has been, at the strong wheel of her house.
The way is clear and she has everything before her.

Perhaps the central paradox of this book is that grandmothers did not suffer the 'identity problems' of their granddaughters. Each woman was unshakably confident about her role, she felt that she had considerable power over her particular sphere of activity, limited though we now consider this to have been. 'The way is clear and she had everything before her' as Lee Knowles puts it. It is today's young women, offered wider choices, who must find their own directions and develop confidence in pursuing them. They no longer have that sense of purpose which came from controlling the fine line between life and death, which was within the province of the women interviewed. They do not have the same cultural mission to rely on for explanations and reasons. Only with difficulty can they control the act of birth or the process of dying within their own homes. Their contact with the elements – with rain water and growing plants – is inessential. The community of the past where there was 'nothing to spare', as the odd jobber's daughter puts it, gave these women a defined sense of purpose, an obviously essential, predetermined role.

In modern times, many agencies outside the family have taken over functions formerly regarded as the prerogative of women in the family. Doctors, nurses, teachers, social workers and other professionals now undertake many of the tasks once done by our great-grandmothers. Reactions to these changes have been both positive and negative. On the positive side, some women overthrow the suppressions sustained by their great-grandmothers. Such suppressions are now seen as merely constraints and burdens, and analysing these as the sources of private pain has been an important step for many women. Freed from being essential exclusively within the family, some women can develop their talents, seek self-improvements or social advancement, thus extending the boundary of their operation from the private to the public world. They no longer need to use marriage as a method of crossing the chalk-line. The distinct datum of their own experiences can be shared with other women in sistership which was denied their great-grandmothers.

On the other hand, the high rates of psychiatric and social breakdown in younger women today suggest that many have been unable to find meaningful lifestyles. Recent studies, such as those outlined by Brown and Harris in their book, *Social Origins of Depression,* have found high rates of depression and other mental disorders among women with young children living in urban settings, particularly those of lower socio-economic classes. Brown and Harris propose that certain things insulate against the loneliness and lack of confidence that contribute to the women's breakdowns: these include having a job and someone to talk to, a confidant. Thus it seems that the alienation of the modern woman differs significantly from the isolation of her great-grandmother. They still suffer the private pain known to their great-grandmothers but without the compensation of knowing that they live in a small world in which they are essential. Marooned in a society which has altered technically and materially beyond recognition, women's work in the family, previously viewed as life-sustaining, can now be done by machines, or more 'professionally' by agents outside the family. Private pain cannot be borne any longer as part of the meaning of a mission. One of the penalties of living in our modern times is emotional and spiritual homelessness. As Peter Berger has pointed out in his book, *Facing up to Modernity* (p.91):

Through most of human history, most human beings have lived in small social settings marked by a plenitude of ongoing face-to-face contacts and by intense solidarity and moral consensus. It would be false to idealize this condition. It was by no means characterized at all times by general happiness; it included every variety of suffering and oppression. But one kind of suffering that it almost never included was what moderns have come to know as alienation, or anomie. Community was real and all-embracing, for better or for worse. The individual was thus rarely, if ever, thrown back upon himself. There were few, if any, uncertainties about the basic cognitive and moral framework of life, hardly any crises of meaning, practically no crises of identity. Individuals knew their world, and they knew who they were. Institutional order, collective meanings, and individual identity were firmly and reliably integrated in the sacred order provided by religious tradition. Human beings were at home in reality – even if, perhaps especially if, this home was often a less than satisfactory place.

The kind of mission felt by the great-grandmothers could only be sustained while their assumptions were shared and reinforced by the community. The private pain was only tolerable because of the overriding sense of purpose presumed by the entire community. Today, a sense of identification with some kind of community – women's or neighbourhood or professional groups – still helps many women deal with their private pain.

It is, after all, the world which has changed the life of women, not the reverse. It is therefore absurd to suggest even implicitly on the basis of this book, that younger women should return to the styles of living of their elders. The women interviewed would not want this and it would be dangerous to advocate it.

On the other hand, we should not dismiss these women of the past as inferior, subordinate nonentities, as some of the feminist literature has tended to do because their lives were confined within the circumference of the family. It is important to realize that women's roles have changed because the meanings formerly attributed to them have disappeared. And the old meanings have disappeared because the social changes which have affected the family have redistributed its functions to other agencies, such as clinic, nursery and school, thus drawing a new boundary between the family and the outside world. It is not surprising that such fundamental alterations in two or three generations should have found many women vulnerable and unprepared.

A similar revolution in the meaning of their destiny will shortly need to be faced by men, who are going to find their essentiality as bread winners challenged and then swept away by a sea of economic and technical changes. This sense of public meaning which has dignified and given purpose to even limited and boring work may disappear, leaving exposed the private pain which most men are now able to suppress behind publicly understood validations of their work.

Now the women of this book, once essential in their world, are old. Their average age is eighty-nine and they are increasingly helpless and unable to control their destinies. The community which their grandchildren dominate has made the old redundant; made them feel that their part lay in the past, their social functions are over. Neither is their experience seen as relevant and useful in today's society, nor is their own community sufficiently intact to offer them support and identity. These old women have managed alone while they could, but when physical or mental frailty, or sheer loneliness, enveloped them, they have been shut away from everyday life into nursing homes, hospitals and hostels for the elderly. They are set apart, and we assume that this is what they want. This process happens everywhere, but in Australia more old people live inside institutions than anywhere in the western world.

While this chapter was being written, two of the women interviewed for the book died and three more were forced to leave their beloved homes and go into hospital. None needs nursing care, but they need protection. To ensure this, they have lost their privacy, their possessions and their independence: of necessity they lead regimented and imprisoned lives in well-intentioned but sterile surroundings. 'It is not death that is so grieving,' wrote Ballanche, 'but decay.' Encapsulated within sagging bodies, the spirits of the women who are confined to hospital suffer. 'I've been here for two years,' said the accountant's daughter, 'but it seems as long as the rest of my life. Every day is like the rest – it's the waiting, it's so empty. Oh, I do wish I was back in the world of busy-ness.' Kate Llewellyn in her poem 'The Aunts', puts it this way:

All my aunts are dying
their bones
in the tissue paper
parcels of their hands

pleat the past
into the edges
of their sheets

they don't flirt now
or pelt each other

with fruit
or toss their heads
at cheeky boys

their red hair
or black
'Straight as a yard
of pumpwater'
as Granny used to say
is grey now
permanently
curled on their pillows

they lie
gesturing vaguely
at their future

which is as clear
as the water
in the glass jug

None of the women in this book likes, or liked, being old. Being removed from everyday life is, in their view, the most common affliction of old age that both caused loneliness and reduced chances to contribute, or to play a part in events. At the same time, few of the women blamed others for their present circumstances. Old age is viewed as one more hurdle to be dealt with within the context of a life of privation. Old age is to be endured and accepted and these women have set about dying in the same practical way they set about living. Most will die alone, separated from family and friends. If they have not come to terms with their separateness in youth, they must face it in old age.

Helplessness is the condition most feared. 'I ask the Lord that he will keep me out of one of those places,' prays the magistrate's daughter. 'What do you think I have done to deserve all this?' wept the blind, deaf and lame accountant's daughter in a most uncharacteristic burst of self-pity. 'I'm not afraid of dying,' said the factory worker's daughter, 'but I am afraid and horrified by the half-death. Please God that I never have to go into one of those places.'

Associated with the feeling of helplessness is another disliked consequence of ageing for these women: the sense of timelessness. This sensation is, of course, much worse for the infirm women in hospital who have much less control of their daily activities than the women living at home. Most of the latter have made strenuous attempts to keep themselves busy and occupied. But for the infirm women, the landscape of endless time which stretched ahead – and behind – was given relief only by the routines of the hospital. The meals, the cups of tea, the drug routines, all assume great significance, because they provide sign posts and landmarks in the undistinguished blur of timelessness. Most of us are able to carry out everyday routines and habits automatically, without noticing them. We wash our faces in the morning, do our hair, wipe the dishes and start the car without being conscious of all the processes involved in each of these actions and movements, partly because these everyday habits are usually the means to an end. But for these women, in the timeless landscape of ageing, the means become the ends: the routines become ways not only of passing the time, but of confirming that time has passed.

In Australia, as in many western countries, hospital care of old people is provided in private nursing homes or in wards for the chronically ill in public hospitals, or in the wards of mental hospitals. In these facilities, the care is second rate compared to the medical and nursing attention given to younger people. Although some staff are concerned and caring, the structures in which they operate are against them. Unsystematic evidence suggests that some of the aged in such institutions are cold, often hungry and socially neglected. One old person, Ellen Newton, kept a diary of her sojourns in private nursing homes in Victoria. Her diaries, published under the title of *This Bed My Centre,* explain her horror at the loss of her liberty and personal responsibility. One of the women in this book explained her feelings about hospitalization:

It's difficult. It's so difficult when they bathe you and dress you. You have male nurses and they don't mind being what I call being cheeky. They go past you and pinch you. One of them did that to me and I said I wouldn't let my own brother do that. I said how old I was. I was more than old enough to be his grandmother. Well, my idea was that they shouldn't treat their own grandmothers with that sort of treatment. But it's so difficult when they bathe you and dress you.

In viewing the treatment of old age as a private pain rather than a public scandal, these women are being true to principles on which they have lived their lives, but we need to ask if it is human of us to exploit this. It is surprising that we, their youngers, do not see the implications in our care of the elderly for our own old age.

Of course the neglect of the old by the young is not uncommon or new: King Lear was not the first to have ungrateful daughters. And the changing structure of our communities has aggravated the problem. Life expectancy has increased, but there are fewer children to look after ageing parents or grandparents. More women work outside the home, thus reducing further the already limited pool of potential caretakers for the aged. So few services exist to support old people staying at home or to help their relatives keep them there that, for many, institutional care is the only expedient. The care of the elderly is neither entirely a family responsibility nor entirely a state matter, but our present system does not reflect the necessary partnership. Either relatives struggle virtually unaided, or old people are hospitalized at great cost to governments. It will require considerable political will to change this.

Meanwhile, being interviewed for this book provided the pleasure of a contribution to the community for a very few old women. Perhaps as we, their descendants, read their stories, we will begin to realize that old people were once young. We may begin to consider what the aged want and what they might offer our communities. At present there is much in our treatment of old people which is reminiscent of those nineteenth-century chalk-lines marking off certain groups as beyond the pale, outside the limits of respectability. 'The old are not us', we keep saying. In our modern world, we have drawn a new line, and the old are on the other side.

Fifteen accounts of daily life are not a history of a period. What these accounts do offer is a series of observations which might provide the beginning assumptions (or the hypotheses) for more detailed social accounting.

How were the women interviewed? Using the conventional research questionnaire would have limited the scope and depth of each individual contribution, at the expense of providing aggregated but superficial information. The interview attempted to cover a series of topics in chronological order from birth to young adulthood. More time was spent in talking about issues in which the women themselves showed special interest or familiarity. So, in theory, a special interview was devised for each woman, but in fact, preconceived plans were often abandoned and surprise 'leads' were followed and many byways explored.

The interview was less of a question–answer exercise than a guided conversation. In attempting to follow the line of thought of each woman very carefully, my main job was to seek further clarification or amplification of matters, to point out and discuss inconsistencies or to ask for reflective comment. This approach was used until a woman's thoughts on a particular topic were exhausted.

The interviews took, on average, between one and a half and three hours. When the age and the frailty of the women is remembered, it must be realized that achieving an interview of this length had some costs: the women could become tired and fail to recall some of the uncomfortable memories. But on the other hand, there was a remarkably high degree of involvement by the women in the interview. Most were not so much talking

227

about their past as actually reliving it and relating back to it. This means that there was a constant dialogue between the woman of the past and the woman of today, an older, wiser woman, interpreting or re-interpreting the event. The distance in time has allowed an active review of the events. There is no such thing as objective or pure recall, as an event or a process is viewed from a woman's vantage point and recalled from a standpoint which makes sense to her subjectively. In technical terms, then, the women's accounts are both reflexive and subjective. (It is for theorists to argue whether or not this constitutes 'history'.)

How were the women selected in the first place? Locating the women was a fairly unsystematic business, achieved usually by introductions from friends or acquaintances. After an introduction, I talked with the woman for about half an hour about the project in general terms. This gave her the opportunity to consider her potential involvement and to give her consent for an interview to be taped. It gave me the chance to decide whether a woman could make a contribution to the book. It was clear that each contributor needed a memory clearly grounded in the present as well as a memory which retained visual and verbal recall of the past in detail. Present-day memory appeared to organize the recollections of the past, and without this, the past dissolved into incoherent fragments. Further, each woman needed the intellectual competence to focus on a restricted period of time in the distant past, to summon up images of the period under question and to transfer these into story form. These demands were a tall order.

It has been estimated that 20 per cent of those over eighty suffer from senile dementia, the prime symptom of which is confusion accompanied by loss of memory. Although in this condition long range memory often lasts longer than immediate recall, *both* types of memory are important to this kind of project. About four women had to be excluded because they lacked the detailed memory to sustain the interview and another three were not interviewed because they lacked the ability to stand outside themselves and to reflect on their personal history. These women appeared to have taken their lives and their circumstances completely for granted and they did not want to project themselves back into the past. They did not want to compare their life with that of other women, nor their present with their past. They were happier to discuss the successes of their children and the potential of their grandchildren than to talk about themselves. They tended to see their lives through the perspective of other people – their husband, their children, their grandchildren – and they did not want their perspective destroyed. It was decided to leave them be.

The interviews in this book were recorded on tape and then transcribed in longhand. The importance of retaining, as far as possible, the texture of the women's pattern of speech seemed to justify this time-consuming job. It also gave a chance to review the themes and topics running through the discussion and to edit out the repetition, pauses and coffee stops which slowed down the story. The contributions of the interviewer have also been deleted. What was rather surprising was the intact way in which the women's contributions stood for themselves after the interviewer's contributions were omitted. All speech used in the accounts is that of the women themselves. There has, however, been some rearrangement of the material in each interview. In an attempt to make each story flow rather than stutter, the material has been consolidated chronologically.

Although the accuracy of the women's memories, in the sense of providing an objective documentary account is not the critical issue, we need to judge the extent to which their memories can be relied on. There was a surprisingly high correspondence between the events they describe (both personal and public) and written primary and secondary sources. This suggests that it is possible to have modest confidence in the reliability of these reports.

Two exceptions will be discussed, largely because they raise wider issues. In the first instance, the grazier's daughter asserts that in her childhood police would stop settlers in the bush to inquire if they were 'bond or free'. Accounts confirm that this routine policy inquiry was made of settlers during the period of convict transportation, 1850 to 1868. Whether this practice existed uniformly, or even occasionally, by the 1890s is not known. The question then is whether the grazier's daughter is recalling not so much her own memory but an image carried over and reinforced by information given her by her parents.

The other example is the description of the accountant's daughter of the politician and ex-convict who grew his hair long to mark the date of his imprisonment. Comparison with written records of the time indicates that this description may not apply to a local convict, as the accountant's daughter implies. More probably it applies to a prominent Western Australian politician, newspaper editor and social reformer of the 1890s. This man emigrated from Cornwall to Queensland, where he founded a labour weekly and was imprisoned subsequently for sedition. His head was shaved when he was put into prison and afterwards he vowed never to cut his hair again. Later, he migrated to Western Australia.

Some say that an oral historian's job is to disentangle the characteristic genres of the life story. Paul Thompson has suggested that there is individual *anecdote*, the family *saga*, the group *legend* and the folk *tale* to distinguish. This implies that it is more important to understand the reason for the construction of certain pieces of information than simply to reject them as objectively inaccurate. For example, many of the women discussed their claims to genteel and even high-born ancestry. The question is not only whether this is true, but what this claim meant to families in the colonial society where one's origins were not obvious. Are these claims a group *legend*, constructed to counter the stigma cast on the colony by the presence of the convicts?

The criteria for accepting or rejecting memories relate more to whether the memories are valid for the person offering them – that is whether they are defensible and well grounded, rather than whether they are pedantically accurate. The obligation of the interviewer is to try to provide a clear channel through which the many sided perceptions which add up to memory can be expressed as clearly as possible. Many social science studies have commented on errors in collecting information due to the memory lapses or the distortions of the respondents. Some of the problems which have been raised can be summarized under the heading of the 'saliency law', that is, events further away in time or of less importance to the individual tend to be forgotten faster. This drawback can be balanced against another tendency, that which Paul Thompson calls 'life review'. This is the tendency of people in old age to want to remember things from their past with a candour which emerges with the perception that life is almost at its end.

The rule which suggests that events further away in the past are less likely to be remembered than those which have taken place recently can be modified if the topics discussed assume some importance and interest to the individual concerned. Thus in achieving the rapport necessary for the oral history interview, the interviewer must stimulate this interest in order to assist the respondent's memory. It is also sometimes possible to construct a practical framework for memory. Centring the interview around certain topics has been discussed, but organization according to time periods is possible too. 'Did that happen while you were still living in that house?' 'Did this really take place before – or was it after – your fiancé went to the war?' These kinds of check questions are mental hatpegs which can be used to 'ground' the information at the interview in real time.

The involvement of the women in their private worlds has already been discussed, along with their isolation from the worlds of politics and economics. Some may consider that this concentration on the private as opposed to the public sphere might have resulted in more discussion about the personal sexual behaviour of the time. But any interviewer of old people knows that this is one of the most difficult areas to broach. Given the isolation of many of these women, what *is* surprising is not the lack of explicit detail as much as the fact that they were prepared to discuss the topic at all. Of course there were differences between individuals on this matter, which related, in part, to personality. And the expectation that the names of the interviewees would be published must have provided another constraint.

Oral historians are not, of course, the only people who try to reconstruct past worlds through the use of childhood memories. The psychoanalyst, the social worker and sometimes the novelist are involved in the process of assembling individual realities and

231

in probing the observations of a child via the adult memory. But the psychoanalyst need make no other claim than that subjective accuracy is the touchstone of significance. In other words, if the patient felt it to be true, it is true. The position of oral historians is more complicated.

But for the women interviewed in this book, the basic question is whether or not their stories have illuminated their period. Their memories are not floodlights across the stage of their time, but neither do they leave their worlds in darkness. Some accounts are luminous; others merely shed light on dim corners. But together, the stories intensify our understanding of a particular period and in that, they have served their purpose.

References

LETTERS

Female Middle Class Emigration Society, Letter Book No. 1, 1862-1876; Letter Book No. 2, 1877-1882; Fawcett Collection, City of London Polytechnic

Letter to Young Women on Leaving England, The Hon. Mrs Joyce, St John's Croft, Winchester, 7th edition, 1913; Fawcett Collection, City of London Polytechnic

JOURNALS

Hecate, A Women's Interdisciplinary Journal (Brisbane), Vol. 1–4, 1975–8

History Workshop, A Journal of Social Historians (Oxford), Vol. 5, 1978

Imperial Colonist, British Women's Emigration Association (London), 1980–1918

Oral History, Oral History Society, University of Essex, Vol. 3 no. 2, 1975

Studies in Western Australian History, Department of History, University of Western Australia, Vol. 1, 1977; Vol. 2, 1978

Time Remembered, The Journal of the Murdoch University History Club, Vol. 1, 1976; Vol. 2, 1978; Vol. 3, 1979

BOOKS

Allen, C., *Plain Tales from the Raj,* André Deutsch, London, 1975

Appleyard, R.T. and T. Manford, *The Beginning: European discovery and early settlement of Swan River, Western Australia,* University of Western Australia Press, Nedlands, W.A., 1979

Austin, A.G. (ed.), *The Webbs' Australian Diary, 1898,* Pitman, Melbourne, 1965

Berger, P.L., *Facing Up to Modernity,* Penguin Books, Harmondsworth, 1979

Biskup, P., *Not Slaves Not Citizens: the Aboriginal problem in Western Australia 1898-1954,* University of Queensland Press, St Lucia, Qld, 1973

Blainey, G., *The Rush That Never Ended: a history of Australian mining,* Melbourne University Press, Melbourne, 1963

Blainey, G., *The Triumph of the Nomads,* Macmillan, Melbourne, 1975

Blainey, G., *Tyranny of Distance,* Macmillan, Melbourne, 1975

Blyth, R., *The View in Winter,* Allen Lane, London, 1979

Blyth, R., *Akenfield: portrait of an English village,* Allen Lane, London, 1969

Bolton, G., *A Fine Country to Starve In,* University of Western Australia Press, Nedlands, W.A., 1972

Borrie, W.D., *Population and Australia: recent demographic trends and their implications,* A.G.P.S., Canberra, 1978

Boyd, M., *The Montforts,* Lansdowne Press, Melbourne, 1975

Bragg, M., *Speak for England,* Hodder and Stoughton, London, 1978

Branca, P., *Silent Sisterhood,* Croom Helm, London, 1975

Brassey, Lady, *The Last Voyage to India and Australia 1886-1887,* Longmans Green and Co., London, 1889

Brittain, V., *Testament of Youth: an autobiographical study of the years 1900-1925,* Virago, London, 1978

Brown, G.W. and T. Harris, *Social Origins of Depression,* Tavistock, London, 1978

Burnett, J. (ed.), *Useful Toil,* Penguin Books, Harmondsworth, 1977

Carnegie, Hon. D., *Spinifex and Sand,* Pearson, London, 1898

Colebatch, H., *A Story of a Hundred Years: Western Australia 1829-1929,* Government Printer, Perth, 1929

Crowley, F.K. and B. de Garis, *A Short History of Western Australia,* Macmillan, Melbourne, 1969

Cowan, P., *A Unique Position: a Biography of Edith Dirksey Cowan 1861-1932,* University of Western Australia Press, Nedlands, W.A., 1978

Daniels, K. and M. Murnane, *Uphill all the Way: a documentary history of women in Australia,* University of Queensland Press, St Lucia, Qld, 1980

Daniels, K., M. Murnane and A. Picot, *Women in Australia: an annotated guide to records,* A.G.P.S., Canberra, 1977

de Beauvoir, S., *Old Age,* André Deutsch, London, 1972

Dixson, M., *The Real Matilda: women and identity in Australia 1788 to 1975,* Penguin, Ringwood, Vic., 1975

Durack, M., *The Rock and the Sand,* Corgi, London, 1971

Durack, M., *To Be Heirs Forever,* Corgi, London, 1976

Evans, G.E., *Where Beards Wag All: the relevance of the oral tradition,* Faber and Faber, London, 1970

Ford, B., *The Elderly Australian,* Penguin Books, Ringwood, Vic., 1979

Garden, D., *Albany,* Nelson, Melbourne, 1977

Hammerton, J., *Emigrant Gentlewomen,* Croom Helm, London, 1979

Hasluck, A., *Portrait with Background: a life, of Georgiana Molloy,* Oxford University Press, Melbourne, 1955

Hasluck, A., *Remembered with Affection,* Oxford University Press, Melbourne, 1963

Hasluck, A., *Unwilling Emigrants: a study of the convict period in Western Australia,* Angus and Robertson, Sydney, 1969

Hasluck, A. and M. Lukis, *Victorian and Edwardian Perth from Old Photographs,* John Ferguson, Sydney 1977

Hughes, M.V., *A London Child of the 1870s,* Oxford University Press, Oxford, 1934

Hughes, M.V., *A London Home in the 1890s,* Oxford University Press, Oxford, 1946

Hunt, L. (ed.), *Westralian Portraits,* University of Western Australia Press, Nedlands, W.A., 1979

Kingston, B., *The World Moves Slowly: a documentary history of Australian women,* Cassell, Sydney, 1977

Kingston, B., *My Wife, My Daughter and Poor Mary Ann,* Nelson, Melbourne, 1975

May, R., *The Gold Rushes: from California to the Klondike,* Macmillan, Melbourne, 1977

Mossenson, D., *State Education in Western Australia 1829-1960,* University of Western Australia Press, Nedlands, W.A., 1972

McCrindle, J. and S. Rowbottam (eds.), *Dutiful Daughters,* Penguin Books, Harmondsworth, 1979

McDonald, P., *Marriage in Australia,* Australian National University Press, Canberra, 1975

Newton, E., *This Bed My Centre,* McPhee Gribble, Melbourne, 1979

Popham, D., *Reflections: profiles of 150 women who helped make Western Australia's history,* Carroll's Ltd, Perth, 1978

Pritchard, K., *The Roaring Nineties,* Jonathan Cape, London, 1946

Rankin, D., *The History of the Development of Education in Western Australia 1829-1923,* Carroll's Ltd, Perth, 1926

Reeves, M.P., *Round About a Pound a Week,* Virago, London, 1979

Salter, E., *Daisy Bates,* Angus and Robertson, Sydney, 1971

Searle, G., *From Deserts the Prophets Come: the creative spirit in Australia 1788-1972,* Heinemann, Melbourne, 1973

Souter, G., *Lion and Kangaroo: Australia 1901-1919,* William Collins, Sydney, 1976

Summers, A., *Damned Whores and God's Police: the colonization of women in Australia,* Penguin Books, Ringwood, Vic., 1975

Stannage, C.T., *The People of Perth: a social history of Western Australia's capital city,* Perth City Council, Perth, 1979

Sutherland, A. and G. Sutherland, *The History of Australia from 1606-1876,* George Robertson and Company, Melbourne, 1878

Taunton, H., *Australind: wanderings in Western Australia and the Malay East,* Edward Arnold, London, 1903

Teale, R., *Colonial Eve: sources on women in Australia 1788-1914,* Oxford University Press, Melbourne, 1978

Thomas, J.E. and A. Stewart, *Imprisonment in Western Australia,* University of Western Australia Press, Nedlands, W.A., 1978

Thompson, F., *Lark Rise to Candleford,* Penguin Books, Harmondsworth, 1973

Thompson, P., *The Edwardians: the remaking of British Society,* Weidenfield and Nicholson, London, 1975

Thompson, P., *The Voice of the Past: oral history,* Oxford University Press, Oxford, 1978

Trollope, A., *South Australia and Western Australia,* Chapman and Hall, London, 1875

Turner, I., *Cinderella Dressed in Yella,* Heinemann Educational, Melbourne, 1969

Women's Migration and Overseas Appointments Society, *New Horizons: 100 years of women's migration,* H.M.S.O., London, 1963

Acknowledgements

Every effort has been made to trace copyright holders, but if any have not been acknowledged, the publisher would be pleased to be informed.

PHOTOGRAPHS

All photographs except those on pages 34, 70, 112, 122, 124 and 192 can be found in the collections of the J.S. Battye Library of West Australian History, Library Board of Western Australia.

p. xiv	Mr William V. Kent, Yokine, W.A.
p. 18	Department of Community Welfare, Perth, W.A.
p. 34	Mrs P. Kynaston Reeves, London
p. 36	Passey Collection, Library Board of Western Australian Department of Agriculture, Perth, W.A.
p. 46	Government Chemical Laboratories, Perth, W.A.
p. 60	Mrs B. Repton, Tammin, W.A.
p. 70	Nottingham County Council Leisure Services Department, U.K.
p. 87	Mrs V. Johnstone, address unknown
p. 112	London Borough of Hackney Library Services
p. 122	Mrs V. Brayley, Swansea, Wales
p. 124	Mrs V. Brayley, Swansea, Wales
p. 144	Mrs B. Repton, Tammin, W.A.
p. 156	Wyalkatchem Shire Council, Wyalkatchem, W.A. West Australian Newspapers Ltd, Perth, W.A.
p. 183	Department of Community Welfare, Perth, W.A.
p. 192	Fellows of Newnham College, Cambridge
p. 193	West Australian Newspapers Ltd, Perth, W.A.

POEMS

Angus and Robertson, Sydney, for:
    'The Old Head Nurse and the Young Marchioness' by Henry Lawson, in
        Henry Lawson: Collected Verse, vol. III, edited by Colin Roderick
    'Betty by the Sea' by Ronald McCuaig in *Quod* by Ronald McCuaig
    'Tangmalangaloo' by John O'Brien in *Around the Boree Log* by John O'Brien

'The Roaring Days' by Henry Lawson in *The Poetical Works of Henry Lawson*
'Paddy's Letter' in *Old Bush Songs* edited by Douglas Stewart and Nancy
    Keesing

University of Queensland Press, St Lucia, Queensland, for:
    'She Speaks' by Judith Rodriquez in *NuPlastic Fanfare Red* (Paper Poets 14)
    by Judith Rodriquez

Fremantle Arts Centre Press, Fremantle, W.A., for:
    'My Grandmother' by Lee Knowles in *Cool Summer* by Lee Knowles

Sisters Publishing Ltd, South Carlton, Victoria, for:
    'Veteran' by Joyce Lee and 'The Aunts' by Kate Llewellyn in *Sisters Poets I*
    edited by R. Dobson

No place for a Nervous Lady
Voices from the Australian Bush

Lucy Frost

'We had no house or hut of any kind of our own, nor
had we even fixed on one particular spot to erect any –
A friend of our's & a Bachelor, (what excellent persons
this poor neglected despised race are!) offered us his
cottage until we should have our own – so to it we went
– Very soon after, we pitched our slab hut on a pretty
flat, close to a nice creek of fresh water –'

Annie Baxter, 1840

Lucy Frost has assembled a fascinating collection of
unpublished and intimate letters and diary entries by
thirteen women in nineteenth century Australia.

Women wrote to keep in touch with their old lives and
to make some kind of private sense of the new. Their
experiences varied widely – from Annie Baxter whose
writings sustained her through a miserable marriage to
a military man and failed farmer, and Ann Williams who
kept a vivid account of a journey with wagon and
bullock team from beyond Queanbeyan to the forest of
Moruya, to Ellen Moger writing from Adelaide to tell
her parents that three of her four young children had
died of starvation on the voyage out.

All would have agreed with Annie Baxter, however,
when after being bled with a penknife, she wrote to her
friend, 'Oh! ye nervous ladies, never come to the bush!'

Double Time
Women in Victoria – 150 Years

edited by Marilyn Lake and Farley Kelly

Few bonuses, but a dual timetable. That's what double time has meant for generations of Australian women.

Here are more than fifty women who have lived in Victoria – convict and nun, actress and soldier settler, writer and housewife, political activist and refugee. Though they have much in common besides multiple responsibilities, their social and personal diversity is striking. But the home, in this study, is as central as the marketplace, reproduction as significant as production.

The book offers a new perspective on history, strongly asserting the place of women and highlighting the relationships between public and private life, paid and unpaid work, government and family, party politics and sexual politics.

For Love or Money

Megan McMurchy, Margot Oliver and Jeni Thornley

A telling and passionate tribute to the unsung labours of
Australian women, past and present. It presents two
hundred years of Australian history through women's
eyes, from the impact of colonisation on Aboriginal
women to the challenges confronting women today.

For Love or Money documents not only the work women
have done in the workplace – the factory, the shop, the
office, the hospital, the school, but also all the work of
caring – as mothers, wives, volunteer workers and in
many other unpaid occupations.

Supporting the authors' incisive analysis is a rich
collection of documentary material, including
photographs, posters, newspaper articles, as well as
letters, diaries, novels, pamphlets, speeches and
interviews never before published.

For Love or Money is a companion work to the film of the
same name.

'a valuable reference book . . . of particular interest in
the enlargement of the concept of "pioneer women" to
include Aboriginal women'
Canberra Times

'informative and thoroughly researched'
Sunday Sun (Brisbane)

Women of the Sun

Hyllus Maris and Sonia Borg

Though they lived in different eras they shared the same resilience and spirit – these Women of the Sun.

ALINTA – she is one of the first to see the men with faces of clay, and one of the few to survive their invasion of the land of the Ancestors.
MAYDINA – she must submit to a new Law, which preaches love while it takes her daughter away.
NERIDA – she seeks the strength to defy tyranny and give her people hope.
LO-ARNA – she discovers the secret of her origin and must come to terms with all that it means.

This quartet of stories speaks with the simplicity and power of the Aboriginal voice, illuminating from their perspective the experience of two centuries of white domination. This is the novel of the award-winning TV series.